Society of Illustrators, Inc.
128 East 63rd Street, New York, NY 10021

ISBN 8230-6055-1
Library of Congress Catalog Card Number 59-10849

Distributors to the trade in the United States
Watson-Guptill Publications
1515 Broadway, New York, NY 10036

Distributed throughout the rest of the world by:
Rotovision, S.A.
9 Route Suisse
1295 Mies, Switzerland

Edited by Jill Bossert
Cover design by Krystyna Skalski
Illustrations by Guy Billout
Interior design by Ryuichi Minakawa
Layout and Production by Naomi Minakawa

Printed in Hong Kong

Photo Credits: Etienne Delessert by Marcel Imsand, Stasys Eidrigevicius by Krzysztof
Szeloch, David Grove by Heather Elmer, B.W. Honeycutt by Erwin Gorostiza, Forbes
Linkhorn by Sandor Acs, Judy Pedersen by Len Irish, Jessie Willcox Smith by Ira L.
Hill, Donald Teague by Terry Morrison, Carol Wald by Trantacoste.

ILLUSTRATORS

1/33
Published by Rotovision S.A. Geneva

PRESIDENT'S MESSAGE

Illustrators 33 continues the tradition of being the official document of record for excellence in the field of American illustration.

For the first time, we have included the size and medium of each piece of art in the catalog copy. This added information, we believe, will be helpful to art directors, as well as to illustrators and art students.

As my term as President comes to a close, I would like to thank Joseph Montebello, Jackie Meyer, and the Publications Committee for their tireless efforts in making this beautiful book a reality.

Also, my sincerest thanks to all the wonderful people who served with me on the Society's Board of Directors. With their very dedicated support we have accomplished a great deal these past two years.

For those of you fortunate enough to be included in *Illustrators 33*, I offer my congratulations. You are now a part of illustration history!

Wendell Minor
President
1989 - 1991
Portrait by Herb Tauss

THE SOCIETY OF ILLUSTRATORS HALL OF FAME

Each year the Society of Illustrators elects to its Hall of Fame those artists who have made an outstanding contribution to the art of illustration throughout the years.

The list of previous winners is truly a "Who's Who" of illustration. Former Presidents of the Society meet annually to elect those who will be so honored.

Short biographies of the recipients of this award, along with examples of their work, are presented in the following pages.

HALL OF FAME 1991

Donald Teague
Jessie Willcox Smith*
William A. Smith*

HALL OF FAME 1958-1990

Norman Rockwell 1958	Edwin Austin Abbey* 1979
Dean Cornwell 1959	Lorraine Fox* 1979
Harold Von Schmidt 1959	Saul Tepper 1980
Fred Cooper 1960	Howard Chandler Christy* 1980
Floyd Davis 1961	James Montgomery Flagg* 1980
Edward Wilson 1962	Stan Galli 1981
Walter Biggs 1963	Frederic R. Gruger* 1981
Arthur William Brown 1964	John Gannam* 1981
Al Parker 1965	John Clymer 1982
Al Dorne 1966	Henry P. Raleigh* 1982
Robert Fawcett 1967	Eric (Carl Erickson)* 1982
Peter Helck 1968	Mark English 1983
Austin Briggs 1969	Noel Sickles* 1983
Rube Goldberg 1970	Franklin Booth* 1983
Stevan Dohanos 1971	Neysa Moran McMein* 1984
Ray Prohaska 1972	John LaGatta* 1984
Jon Whitcomb 1973	James Williamson* 1984
Tom Lovell 1974	Robert Weaver 1985
Charles Dana Gibson* 1974	Charles Marion Russell* 1985
N.C. Wyeth* 1974	Arthur Burdett Frost* 1985
Bernie Fuchs 1975	Al Hirschfeld 1986
Maxfield Parrish* 1975	Rockwell Kent* 1986
Howard Pyle* 1975	Maurice Sendak 1987
John Falter 1976	Haddon Sundblom* 1987
Winslow Homer* 1976	Robert T. McCall 1988
Harvey Dunn* 1976	René Bouché* 1988
Robert Peak 1977	Pruett Carter* 1988
Wallace Morgan* 1977	Erté 1989
J.C. Leyendecker* 1977	John Held Jr.* 1989
Coby Whitmore 1978	Arthur Ignatius Keller* 1989
Norman Price* 1978	Burt Silverman 1990
Frederic Remington* 1978	Robert Riggs* 1990
Ben Stahl 1979	Morton Roberts* 1990
	Presented posthumously

HALL OF FAME COMMITTEE

Willis Pyle/*Chairman*
Participating Past Presidents of the Society:
Stevan Dohanos, Charles McVicker, Howard Munce, Alvin J. Pimsler, Warren Rogers, Shannon Stirnweis, Diane Dillon

Donald Teague came to illustration by way of the Art Students League where he studied with Frank V. DuMond in 1915. Upon completing his studies he turned to architecture as a career but he changed to illustration because it was less mechanical and more interesting. His first job was doing car cards, posters, and lettering for Ward & Gow, an art service. More interested than ever in making pictures, he returned to the League to hone his skills.

His new career was interrupted by a stint in the Navy which he spent cruising the Caribbean. On Armistice Day, 1918, Teague returned to New York where he got a job illustrating two stories for the *Delineator* magazine. After this he had no jobs for a long time, having gone to spend time on a working ranch in Colorado and discovering on his return to New York that art editors wait for no one. Then Arthur McKeogh, the art editor for *The Saturday Evening Post,* gave him his first story for that magazine and Teague never had to ask for another job.

Until 1923 he illustrated in oil. Then he went to England on a sketching trip to visit English horse fairs which he sketched in watercolor. Upon his return he showed them to Howard Quinan, the editor of *Collier's,* who suggested that from this point on Teague paint in that medium. It was a turning point in his career, the beginning of a love affair between an artist and his medium. Through many years of working with watercolor, Teague never tired of it, perhaps because it possesses the quality he called "verve." His journeys abroad in the '20s were valuable sources of the original material upon which he has always insisted.

The next step was a move to New Rochelle, New York, which, at the time, was a community of illustrators headed by Norman Rockwell and J.C. Leyendecker. Also in residence were Al Parker, Mead Schaeffer, and Tom Lovell who, along with Peter Helck, Walter Biggs, Stevan Dohanos, John LaGatta, Dean Cornwell, C.C. Beall, N.C. Wyeth, and Harold Von Schmidt, would become the leaders in the field.

Teague developed his technique with the advice and counsel of Dean Cornwell, who never refused to look at and, if necessary, criticize his pictures. Teague credits Cornwell as the single most important influence on his illustrating career.

Teague married Verna Timmins and moved to Los Angeles in 1938. Bill Chessman, who was then *Collier's* editor, concluded that if the artist was going to live in California he could paint Western subjects, popular editorial fare at the time. Living in Encino, Teague found himself in a center for Western lore provided by the movie industry, which at that time was producing a large number of Western films. The cowboys he met in Hollywood, who worked as actors and stuntmen in the '30s and early '40s, were insistent upon authenticity. They took an intense personal interest in seeing that Teague got it all perfect—down to riding wrinkles in the right spots and dressing his picture cowboys in the proper order—the hat before anything else.

His illustrating career was at its height when, in 1958, *Collier's* stopped publication. After 38 active and highly successful years in illustration, Teague saw this event as an omen and left illustrating completely to concentrate solely on painting landscapes in watercolor. Since then, his work has been exhibited in the Metropolitan Museum of Art; National Academy of Design; Royal Watercolor Society, London; Tokyo Museum; Art Institute, Chicago; and many others. Recognition of his abilities has garnered him every major prize in the field and inclusion in public and private collections from Oklahoma City to Peking.

Teague paints from dark to light. He tries for a dramatic effect whenever possible. The idea of trying to produce quality is dominant, along with a need for originality. His favorite subjects include anything outdoors, especially water and skies, and figures. His method combines firsthand observation with high emotions and work done in the studio.

Speaking today he says, "The type of illustration and advertising prevalent in those days doesn't exist now. In those days some of illustration was done by artists whose aim was to come close to fine art in technique. Illustrators could outpaint the painters any day of the week. An illustrator had to reach a certain quality of production or he wasn't accepted. He had to really know his craft."

Tom Lovell, the artist's friend and fellow Society of Illustrators Hall of Fame member, said, "Donald Teague stresses the prime importance of content, otherwise defined as the substance or the matter of the thing at hand. Anyone who has followed his works knows that he has lived by this tenet...[His illustrations] are always strong in design and intriguing in the portrayal of a situation, the vital ingredient needed to persuade the browser to become a reader."

Linda Teague Key

from an interview with her father in May, 1991

Illustration from "Under the Burning Sky" by H.A. DeRosso, *Collier's*,
June 6, 1953. This piece was signed "Edwin Dawes" which was the
pseudonym Teague used for a time so he could work for competing
magazines.

HALL OF FAME 1991
JESSIE WILLCOX SMITH (1863-1935)

Courtesy Illustration House

The subject of children and their mothers was never more beautifully idealized than by Jessie Willcox Smith. In illustration after illustration she showed the dignified tenderness of a woman's love for her child. Through her empathy and artistic and compositional skills, Smith's identification with the children themselves is unparalleled in illustration, although she had no notion of her gifts when she began her adult life. By the time she was seventeen she was teaching kindergarten and only a fortuitous invitation by an artistic cousin introduced her to the possibility of her talent. Acting as chaperone while her cousin gave art instruction to a young professor who, after two frustrating attempts abandoned his lessons, Jessie discovered the joy of drawing. She stopped teaching and enrolled at Mrs. Sarah Peter's School of Design for Women in Philadelphia, the city where she had been born on September 6, 1863.

In 1885 she continued her training at the Pennsylvania Academy of the Arts where she studied briefly under Thomas Eakins. Finding the atmosphere too dour and the students filled with too studied a seriousness, she left to take up illustration professionally in 1888. It was, at the time, one of the few professions available to genteel, "surplus" women—the unmarried and widowed. It was also a vocation in which she could combine her love of children with her talent as an artist. This was a time when it appeared that few men could draw children well and few women could depict anything but. Smith's first published illustration appeared in the May 1888 edition of *St. Nicholas Magazine*, a thrilling experience for her. She was financially reliant on the advertising illustrations she did for *Ladies' Home Journal*. Although it was not the type of

work for which she would become famous, it proved to be excellent professional experience.

The person who most influenced her work and generations of illustrators, entered her life in 1894. As one of Howard Pyle's first students at Drexel Institute in Philadelphia, she found that the force of his spirit and overall inspirational view of the art of illustration shaped the way she created pictures thereafter. She discovered that when she composed a piece, after careful consideration of the story and characters, she could imagine what they were doing and was bound to get the right composition because she had "lived these things."

Pyle was responsible for Smith's and classmate Violet Oakley's first major illustration assignment: Longfellow's *Evangeline*. The lifelong friendship forged with Oakley and another Pyle student, Elizabeth Shippen Green, led to a long period when the three shared studio and living spaces. What began as a sensible budgetary arrangement for the youthful illustrators became a seemingly idyllic, cooperative, creative atmosphere of "a band of independent partners in talent who have no time for rivalries." The artists, some of their relations and Henrietta Cozens, an avid gardener, shared several beautiful homes, most notably "Cogslea" where they lived until 1911 when Elizabeth Shippen Green married. Smith then moved to nearby "Cogshill" where she lived until her death in 1935.

As one of the country's most successful illustrators, Smith augmented her substantial income with private portrait commissions. Her work, executed primarily in charcoal, watercolor, and gouache, appeared in most of the popular magazines including *Century, Collier's, Good Housekeeping, Scribner's,* and *Woman's Home Companion.* Her many books became classics, all of which were for or about children: Robert Louis Stevenson's *A Child's Garden of Verses, The Book of the Child, The Water Babies, Heidi, Little Women,* and *The Jessie Willcox Smith Mother Goose,* among others.

She had a charming technique for achieving the natural look in her young models, all of whom were the children of friends, whom she would observe in the lovely settings of her home and garden "and try to get them to take unconsciously the positions that I happened to want for a picture." Then she would tell them fairy tales with great animation while she painted. She said, "a child will always look directly at someone who is telling them a story."

In this cynical world, it is difficult to imagine that motherhood and children could have been perceived in so innocent and idealized a manner as those depicted by Jessie Willcox Smith, but from her own descriptions of her feelings and by contemporary reports, she remained "a grown person who retains the frank sweetness of a child...whose own personality is not less lovely and imaginative and unaffected than that of the children she charms with fairy-stories."

Jill Bossert

"Little Miss Muffet," *Good Housekeeping Magazine,* January 1913.
Courtesy of American Illustrators Gallery/Judy Goffman Fine Art.

WILLIAM A. SMITH, N.A. (1918-1989)

Bill Smith had a precocious and prodigious art talent; he started early and just kept growing. In his long career he excelled in everything he did and collected an extraordinarily long list of honors and awards. His efforts were almost equally divided between teaching, painting for exhibition, and illustrating for books, magazines, and advertising clients. Along the way, he also explored print-making and painted murals. The youngest artist to be elected president of the American Watercolor Society, he was also a National Academician and served a three-year term as president of the International Association of Art, the organization of painters, sculptors, and graphic artists of seventy nations affiliated with UNESCO. He travelled extensively on various projects including a State Department lecture tour in Japan with an exhibit of his work that drew an average of 10,000 viewers a day.

Smith's paintings are in the Metropolitan Museum of Art in New York, the Los Angeles Museum, the Air Force Academy and many other collections. He exhibited in nearly every important museum in the United States and in more than twenty one-man shows abroad, including Italy, Greece, Japan, the Philippines, and Turkey.

This career all began with his studies at the University of Toledo and Keane's Art School in Toledo. Upon arrival in New York at nineteen, he soon found work doing comic strip art and pulp illustrations while he studied further at the Grand Central School of Art. By 1942 he had obtained his first illustration commission from *Cosmpolitan* magazine.

As an illustrator, Smith's art was distinguished by its painterly quality and excellent draftsmanship. In his black-and-white work, he developed the use of the Oriental tusche on gesso panel into which he often cut or scraped the surface for a scratchboard effect. His color, both in oils and watercolor, was rich and strong. He preferred to paint on locale from life, and his figures were always convincing and expressive.

Many of his story assignments had international backgrounds, and he was particularly effective with drama and suspense when he was teamed up with authors of spy thrillers. He was expertly equipped for this subject matter as a result of his World War II experience with the Office of Strategic Services in China doing psychological warfare projects. Among his many magazine clients were *The Saturday Evening Post, Redbook, Cosmoplitan, True, This Week, Life,* and *The Reader's Digest.* He also painted for many advertisers, among them the outstanding series for the John Hancock Mutual Life Insurance Company.

Smith was simultaneously painting illustrations and for exhibition on a regular basis. He received numerous honors including the Obrig Prize for oil painting, the Ranger Fund Purchase, Pennell Memorial purchase, Winslow Homer Memorial Prize, twice winner of the National Academy Prize, $1,000 Grand Prize and Gold Medal for Watercolor from the American Watercolor Society and many others. He also lectured at numerous art institutions in the United States and abroad.

The poet, Carl Sandburg, who had posed for a portrait by the artist, paid this tribute to William A. Smith: "When he paints bug, leaf, animal, antique head, old worn house or fresh child face, his prayer is to be inside of it as part of what gives it personal identity and inviolable dignity."

Walt Reed

Illustration House

"He made a frozen frontier tell its secrets..." Portrait of Richard E. Byrd,
advertisement for John Hancock Mutual Life Insurance Company.
Courtesy of Illustration House.

HAMILTON KING AWARD

The Hamilton King Award is presented each year for the best illustration of the year by a member of the Society of Illustrators. The selection is made by former recipients of this award.

HAMILTON KING AWARD 1965-1990

Paul Calle 1965
Bernie Fuchs 1966
Mark English 1967
Robert Peak 1968
Alan E. Cober 1969
Ray Ameijide 1970
Miriam Schottland 1971
Charles Santore 1972
Dave Blossom 1973
Fred Otnes 1974
Carol Anthony 1975
Judith Jampel 1976
Leo & Diane Dillon 1977

Daniel Schwartz 1978
William Teason 1979
Wilson McLean 1980
Gerald McConnell 1981
Robert Heindel 1982
Robert M. Cunningham 1983
Braldt Bralds 1984
Attila Hejja 1985
Doug Johnson 1986
Kinuko Y. Craft 1987
James McMullan 1988
Guy Billout 1989
Edward Sorel 1990

HAMILTON KING AWARD 1991
BRAD HOLLAND b. 1943

From an interview with long-time friend, Wendell Minor:

Wendell Minor: Twenty years ago we came to one of these Annual Shows and before the afternoon was over, you'd gotten both of us kicked out. Remember?

Brad Holland: They were pretty mad at me, weren't they?

WM: You were insisting they take your work out of the exhibition. I didn't think they'd ever let us back in.

BH: So now you're President, see?

WM: Ironic, isn't it?

BH: How does it feel to be leaving office? Did you have time to leave your mark?

MW: I certainly got some people to join who swore they never would. You're not going to quit after I step down, are you?

BH: Well, I have a feeling pretty soon they're gonna remember where they've seen us before and kick us out again.

WM: Alright, so now you've won the Hamilton King Award. How does that feel?

BH: You know how I feel about awards, right? They're great, but you could win a Nobel Prize for art and it wouldn't help you paint your next picture. You'd just have to start over the next day with a white piece of paper. Only you've used up much of your originality in your past work. At best, awards are like locks when you go through a canal. They seal off what you can't go back to.

WM: So is this picture symbolic of your career in some way? Your career has been very segmented. You've worked in different styles; taken different approaches.

BH: Actually, the picture may symbolize that I work best with a long deadline.

WM: Why do you say that?

BH: Well, about 1970 I did a little black-and-white drawing and it didn't pan out, so I abandoned it. Then, twenty years later, this image just drifted into my head, like out of a mist. All the problems were solved. A kind of improved version.

WM: So you're saying it took twenty years to complete a sketch?

BH: Any art directors out there, place your orders early.

WM: How long did it take you to paint it?

BH: A couple of hours.

WM: What is the painting's theme? Does it have a title?

BH: "I'm Coming Apart."

WM: It's ironic that you won two Gold Medals this year for other pieces. One, in fact, in the same category as this painting. Do you think there's a reason why this didn't receive a Gold Medal but was picked for the Hamilton King?

BH: Well, the other pictures were experiments with crayons and sloppy drawing. One was an experiment to see how I'd paint a crowd. This deal here was a purely interior picture. Some pictures start out fuzzy and come into focus. Some start as one thing and end up as something else. As I said, this one came all worked out in my head. I just went in and got it.

WM: It's a very grave painting. Some of your pictures are more realistic.

BH: Yeah, but this one is even more realistic than those. This one doesn't prove anything. There's no charm to it. It doesn't invite you in. It's so homely. It looks like it was painted with mud. Using a putty knife. Who's going to like it except for itself.

WM: What were you thinking when you painted it?

BH: I don't remember thinking anything. It was like being an electric cord with current running through you.

MW: How was this different from the 1971 version?

BH: That was an ink drawing. A man was having his arms and legs torn off by people who didn't have any. I did pictures like that back then. I did it for myself. It was a drawing of a guy who had turned himself into spare parts for just anybody. It was too personal a picture to be any good. It took twenty years for all the psychological details to fade away and the meaningless elements to come forward.

MW: I'd think you'd want a picture to communicate as much meaning as possible.

BH: No. I want to strip a picture of everything but the force behind it.

WM: Do you find as you grow older that you need fewer elements in a painting?

BH: Well, less of what the eye sees.

WM: What you see in your mind's eye?

BH: I'm kind of nearsighted. So I'm not always sure of what I see with my regular eyes.

WM: Nearsighted people are supposed to be introspective. Do you consider yourself shy?

BH: I'm OK after I've been introduced. But I'd never be much of a Shriner...I've always wondered which artists would be Shriners and which wouldn't. Rubens would have been. So would Van Dyke and Reynolds. Jackson Pollack was a closet Shriner.

WM: And Picasso.

BH: Do you suppose? Picasso would have been laughs at a

Wendell Minor, Steven Heller, Brad Holland, 1971

"I'm Coming Apart," a promotional poster for a lecture series at the Art Directors Club of Cincinnati

convention alright, but he was very weird. I have a feeling the Shriners would have begged him to join and then encouraged him not to attend meetings. Braque would have been a Mason.

WM: Not unless he was the highest degree.

BH: Right. Name some modern artists.

WM: Wyeth. Hopper. Hopper wouldn't have been a Shriner. But N.C. Wyeth had the making of one.

BH: I thought the Wyeths were a lodge by themselves. You mean I can't join?

WM: Rembrandt would have been a Shriner.

BH: Do you think so? I think he's a problem. He painted all those people in turbans and harem pants, though, didn't he? But I have a feeling Rembrandt wanted to be a Shriner and hated himself for it. You can see it in the self-portraits. In half of them he's a man of sorrows and acquainted with grief and in the other half he looks like a guy who'd say, "Meet the wife." He's a problem alright.

WM: What about you? What lodge would Brad Holland belong to?

BH: Is the Raccoon Lodge in Brooklyn? Or is that the Mystic Knights of the Sea?

SPECIAL AWARDS 1991

Among those honored by the Society of Illustrators in 1991 were two people who made substantial contributions to the illustration profession. David K. Stone received the Dean Cornwell Recognition Award for his efforts in organizing the Society of Illustrators Annual of American Illustration 33 years ago. Dean Ellis was presented the Arthur William Brown Achievement Award for his continuing efforts on behalf of the goals and ideals of the Society of Illustrators.

The industry is indebted to the recipients of these awards for helping to raise the profession's and public's awareness and appreciation of the art of illustration.

THE ARTHUR WILLIAM BROWN ACHIEVEMENT AWARD 1991
DEAN ELLIS

A primary reason the Society of Illustrators has existed since 1901 is that, on rare occasions, we gain a member who willingly accepts the difficult, often unrewarding SI chores with the necessary firmness and tenacity to achieve positive results.

Dean Ellis has performed this role with distinction since 1958. The ink was hardly dry on his membership certificate when he was recruited to help conduct a survey on the nature of the Society's membership.

During the next 20 years he served in several key positions on the Executive Committee. As Vice President to two Presidents he often had to fill their office for extensive periods, including a time when he narrowly avoided a lawsuit against the Society and another when he assumed the duties of the Annual Exhibition when the chairman was unable to continue.

Because of his obvious leadership abilities, Dean was repeatedly asked to accept the presidency of the Society of Illustrators. But he always refused, preferring to take on tasks such as representative to the Joint Ethics Committee in 1965, sitting in judgement of the differences between artist and buyer.

In 1968 Ellis moved into the Treasurer's office where he stayed for ten years. During this time, the Board struggled to pay bills, deal with double-digit inflation, and for two-and-a-half years, manage the "200 Years of American Illustration" show and book. While not without its problems, this show was, without a doubt, one of the most important and significant efforts undertaken by the Society.

Dean was asked to return as Treasurer in 1987, a position he currently holds while also conducting the Life/Senior Membership, the Welfare Fund, and the Finance Committees.

All these contributions are conducted in much the same manner as he creates his art, with a good deal of intelligence, craft and creativity. If we had to pay for these services we would, no doubt, find it necessary to double the dues.

David K. Stone
President 1967-1968

THE DEAN CORNWELL RECOGNITION AWARD 1991
DAVID K. STONE

It's proper, as the cliché has it, for one to "pay his dues" on the way up. David Stone, the 30th President of the Society, who has received this year's Dean Cornwell Recognition Award, paid his during an exciting and innovative period in the middle '50s.

He became a member in '54 and arrived with a head of steam and quickly made it evident that he was there to *take part.*

Having a love for parliamentary procedure and fortified by a stentorian voice that combined the qualities of Everett Dirksen, Carl Sandburg, and Ethel Merman, he was committee-bound from the start.

His first responsibility was as Education Committee Chairman where he enlisted the aid of the likes of Von Schmidt, Prohaska, and Dorne to regularly speak to students of the New York Arts & Science High School.

Any job well done at the Society will soon get you another job to do well; hence he was elected Vice President. He then initiated a Luncheon Speakers Series to bring culture and cash to the noon hour. It did.

As a co-chairman of the Hanging Committee he was one of many who noted that photography was making a disastrous dent in illustration, as each Art Directors Show revealed. So the idea of an Annual Show of Illustration occurred. It took a long year of trial, groping, and endless meetings between 60 members, 11 sub-committees, and 25 jurors to thrash out the procedures needed to mount the first show. The amount of midnight oil expended rivaled the fires of Kuwait.

His shepherding of this seminal project is the prime reason for being dubbed for the Cornwell Award.

In '67 he was elected President and instigated the re-design of the luncheon area and the reconstruction of the Main Gallery with the designer, Ko Domoto.

He also started the Fund Development Program and worked on the Life and Senior Membership Committees, which were separate at the time.

The five people who sponsored him for Society membership long ago seem to have known what they were doing.

Howard Munce
President 1955-1956

CHAIRMAN'S MESSAGE

Two of the more interesting things about chairing Illustrators 33 were the overnights I spent behind the red door at 128 East 63rd Street. After long days filled with more caffeine than was prudent, preparing the piles of entries for the jury, viewing endless slides of unpublished work, I'd lie awake, exhausted, listening to the creaks and croaks—the ghosts of illustrators?—in the old building. Aside from being scared, I also missed two games in the World Series.

Being so involved in the process removed some of the mystique, but also revealed some interesting aspects of the jurying process. In the Advertising and Institutional categories especially, the larger and more lushly printed the images, the more attention they received. Also, juries tended to select what they're familiar with—what's safe and proven award-worthy. One juror felt he was the one who most deserved a medal and I found myself, gently, reminding him that he was disqualified. Some jurors—especially the artists who were also educators—were more avant garde in their choices, more interested in pushing the limits.

Some unexpected aspects of the process struck me. Delightfully, I felt an incredible sense of comradery with my Assistant Chairman, John Thompson, and working with Herb Tauss on the poster was very gratifying. I also found myself thinking in diplomatic ways that were not so familiar to me.

Since I was in school, I considered the Annual the Bible, the way I got a handle on the profession. Now, having worked on it (and wondered, like Groucho Marx, if they let me do this, how special is it?) I feel that the judges

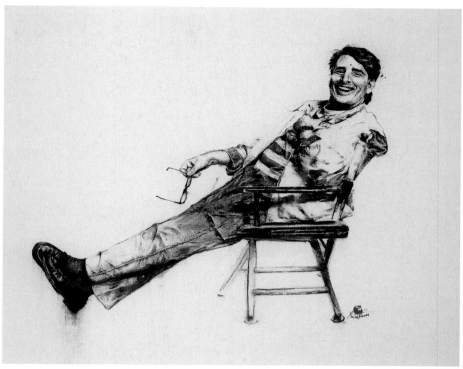

took their work very seriously. It's a magical book. It's an honest book.

[signature]

Peter Fiore
Chairman, 33nd Annual Exhibition
Portrait by Herb Tauss

JURYING THE ANNUAL EXHIBITION: HOW IT WORKS

The most important function of the Annual Exhibition Past Chairmen's Committee is the selection of jurors, which takes place approximately seven months prior to the actual jurying.

A large blackboard is set up with five vertical columns—four for the categories (Advertising, Editorial, Book & Institutional) and one in which to list diverse types of jurors. Every effort is made to create a good mix of talented illustrators and art directors with a wide range of tastes.

The first jurors selected are four Society of Illustrator members, each of whom acts as chairman of one of the categories. Eight additional jurors, including non-Society members, are then selected for each category. In order to avoid bias, jurors are placed in categories other than those from which their primary income is derived professionally. A period of three years must elapse before a juror may serve again. Jurors may not win awards in the category they are judging.

Jurying takes place during four days in October—one category each day. All published entries are set out in stacks of black-and-white, 2-color, full color, and are also broken down according to size within that framework.

After the jurors have completed viewing all the entries and have marked those which they feel qualify for the show, the staff sorts them into groups of "like" votes and those with the highest are brought back to be considered for awards.

During the initial voting, jurors are asked to vote silently, without discussion, but when the selection of awards gets underway, jurors are free to express their views on why they think a certain piece merits an award.

The unpublished entries, submitted in slide form, are projected on a screen and voted on by means of a unique voting machine which enables each juror to cast his vote privately. Awards for unpublished pieces are selected the following week by the Balancing Jury.

The Balancing Jury is composed of the current Exhibition Chairman, the four Category Chairmen, and two Past Chairmen. Since each artist accepted in the show is allowed no more than three pieces in a category and no more than five in the entire show (not counting award-winning pieces), it is the Balancing Jury's responsibility to whittle down those exceeding this number.

The Society of Illustrators takes great pride in the integrity with which this show has been managed over the years and intends to maintain this high standard.

Arpi Ermoyan

EDITORIAL JURY

Alvin J. Pimsler
CHAIRMAN, ILLUSTRATOR

Jim Barkley
ILLUSTRATOR

Bascove
ARTIST

Bob Deschamps
ARTIST, ILLUSTRATOR

William Gregory
ART DIRECTOR, *READER'S DIGEST*

David Grove
ILLUSTRATOR

Judy Pedersen
ILLUSTRATOR

Neal Pozner
NEAL POZNER DESIGN

David Tommasino
ART DIRECTOR, SCHOLASTIC, INC.

AWARD WINNERS

Gary Kelley
GOLD MEDAL

———————————

Gary Kelley
SILVER MEDAL

———————————

Wendell Minor
SILVER MEDAL

———————————

John Jude Palencar
SILVER MEDAL

EDITORIAL

"The magazine wanted an exciting illustration for a fiction piece. Originally, I rendered the man without his pants on...I thought that was exciting. The art director also thought that was exciting. It scared the editor. We put pants on the man. Paranoia!"

1

ARTIST: **GARY KELLEY**

ART DIRECTOR: Barbara Chilenskas, Kati Korpijaakko

CLIENT: Glamour Magazine

MEDIUM: Pastel on Paper

SIZE: 22x18

"Actually, this is a book illustration. It was done for a Guy de Maupassant story. *Step-by-Step Graphics* photographed me while I was working on it. Very distracting. But I guess I shouldn't complain. It won a medal. I must admit, I like it when I win medals."

2

ARTIST: **GARY KELLEY**
ART DIRECTOR: Gary Kelley
CLIENT: Step-by-Step Graphics
MEDIUM: Pastel on Paper
SIZE: 28x22

WENDELL MINOR

Born in Aurora, Illinois, Wendell Minor was graduated from the Ringling School of Art and Design in Sarasota, Florida. Well known in the publishing industry for the paintings he has done for the jackets of many best selling novels, he is the recipient of over 200 professional awards. In 1988 Minor was chosen as one of a six-member team commissioned by NASA to capture the spirit of the Shuttle Discovery's Return to Flight at the Kennedy Space Center. He was also commissioned by the United States Postal Service to design the Centennial stamp celebrating North Dakota's one hundred years of statehood.

3
ARTIST: **WENDELL MINOR**
ART DIRECTOR: Judy Garlan
CLIENT: The Atlantic Monthly
MEDIUM: Acrylic on Masonite
SIZE: 21x21

JOHN JUDE PALENCAR

A graduate of Columbus College of Art and Design, John is primarily a book illustrator for such clients as Time/Life Books, Bantam, Dell, Doubleday, Simon & Schuster. An expanding list of clients includes Anheuser-Busch and Paramount Pictures. His work has been accepted in numerous Society of Illustrators Annuals, Communication Arts Illustration Annuals, Print Regional Design Annuals, and others.

4

ARTIST: **JOHN JUDE PALENCAR**

ART DIRECTOR: Tina Adamek

CLIENT: Postgraduate Medicine

MEDIUM: Watercolor on Board

SIZE: 29x30

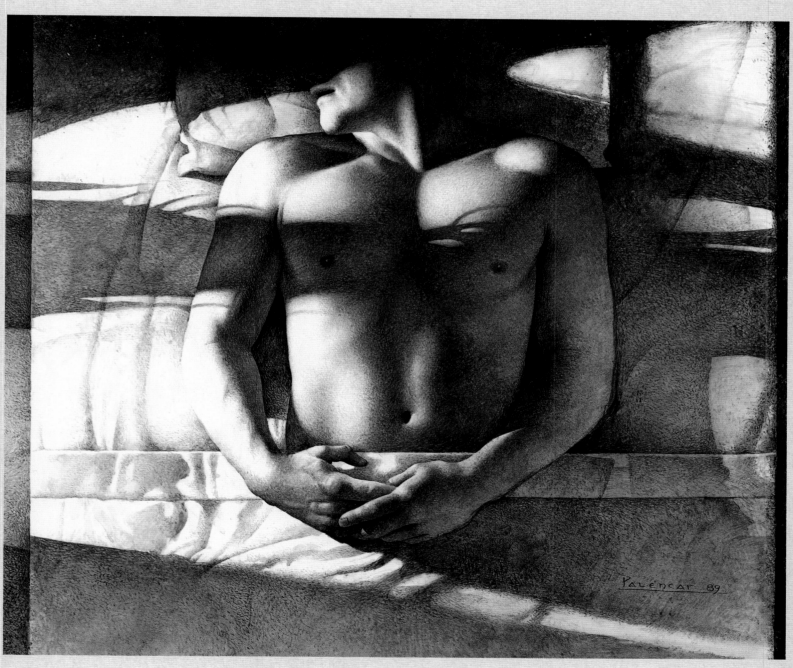

5

ARTIST: **BURT SILVERMAN**

ART DIRECTOR: Theodore Kalomirakis

CLIENT: American Heritage

MEDIUM: Oil on Canvas

SIZE: 20x24

6

ARTIST: **BURT SILVERMAN**

ART DIRECTOR: Bill Cadge

CLIENT: Think

MEDIUM: Watercolor, Pastel on Board

SIZE: 14x22

7

ARTIST: **BURT SILVERMAN**

ART DIRECTOR: Bill Cadge

CLIENT: Think

MEDIUM: Oil on Canvas

SIZE: 30x40

8

ARTIST: **BILL MAYER**

ART DIRECTOR: Wanda D. Maioresco

CLIENT: Travel & Leisure

MEDIUM: Gouache, Dyes

SIZE: 10x12

5

6

7

8

9

ARTIST: **PHIL BOATWRIGHT**

ART DIRECTOR: Naomi Trujillo

CLIENT: Discipleship Journal

MEDIUM: Acrylic, Oil, Prisma Color

SIZE: 24x21

10

ARTIST: **MICHAEL PARASKEVAS**

ART DIRECTOR: Alyson Walsh

CLIENT: Dan's Paper

MEDIUM: Acrylic on Canvas

SIZE: 54x66

11

ARTIST: **MARVIN MATTELSON**

ART DIRECTOR: Richard Bleiweiss

CLIENT: Penthouse

MEDIUM: Acrylic

SIZE: 22x19

12

ARTIST: **MARVIN MATTELSON**

ART DIRECTOR: Richard Bleiweiss

CLIENT: Penthouse

MEDIUM: Acrylic

SIZE: 21x18

9

10

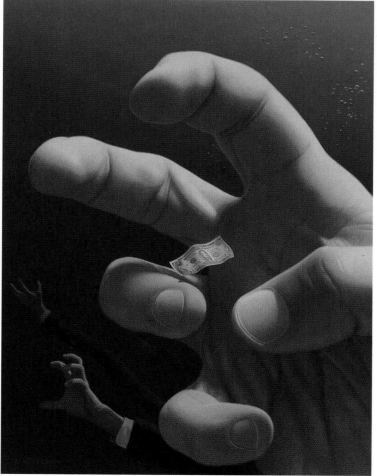

11

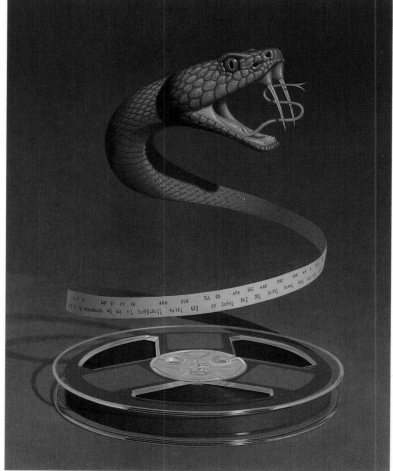

12

13

ARTIST: **HIRO KIMURA**

ART DIRECTOR: Hiro Kimura

MEDIUM: Mixed Media

SIZE: 20x20

14

ARTIST: **SALLY WERN COMPORT**

ART DIRECTOR: Beth Ceisel

CLIENT: Consumer Digest, Inc.

MEDIUM: Charcoal, Pencil on Paper

SIZE: 12x16

15

ARTIST: **MARK SUMMERS**

ART DIRECTOR: Steve Heller

CLIENT: The New York Times Book Review

MEDIUM: Scratchboard

SIZE: 6x4

16

ARTIST: **MARK SUMMERS**

ART DIRECTOR: Steve Heller

CLIENT: The New York Times Book Review

MEDIUM: Scratchboard

SIZE: 6x6

14

15

16

17
ARTIST: **RICK BERRY**
2nd ARTIST: **PHIL HALE**
ART DIRECTOR: David Carson
CLIENT: Beach Culture
MEDIUM: Oil on Watercolor Paper
SIZE: 25x20

18
ARTIST: **MARK PENBERTHY**
ART DIRECTOR: Brenda Van Ginkel
CLIENT: Toronto Life
MEDIUM: Oil on Watercolor Paper
SIZE: 22x28

19
ARTIST: **RAPHAELLE GOETHALS**
ART DIRECTOR: Gabrielle Raumberger
CLIENT: Geffen Company
MEDIUM: Acrylic on Board
SIZE: 14x10

20
ARTIST: **DAVID LEVINSON**
ART DIRECTOR: Jennifer Cole
CLIENT: Scholastic Search Magazine
MEDIUM: Oil on Masonite
SIZE: 20x15

17

18

19

20

21

ARTIST: **KUNIO HAGIO**

ART DIRECTOR: Richard Bleiweiss

CLIENT: Penthouse

MEDIUM: Mixed Media on Board

SIZE: 28x22

22

ARTIST: **KUNIO HAGIO**

ART DIRECTOR: Mike Rizzo

CLIENT: University of Illinois/Commerce Magazine

MEDIUM: Oil on Board

SIZE: 22x30

23

ARTIST: **KINUKO Y. CRAFT**

ART DIRECTOR: Judy Garlan

CLIENT: The Atlantic Monthly

MEDIUM: Watercolor on Paper

SIZE: 22x16

24

ARTIST: **NICHOLAS WILTON**

ART DIRECTOR: Bob Eisner

CLIENT: Newsday Magazine

MEDIUM: Acrylic

SIZE: 15x12

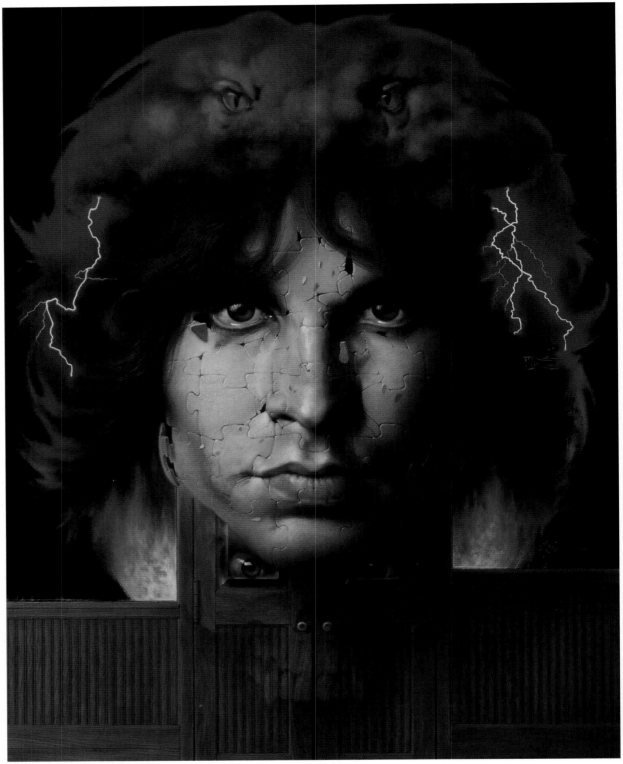

21

22

23

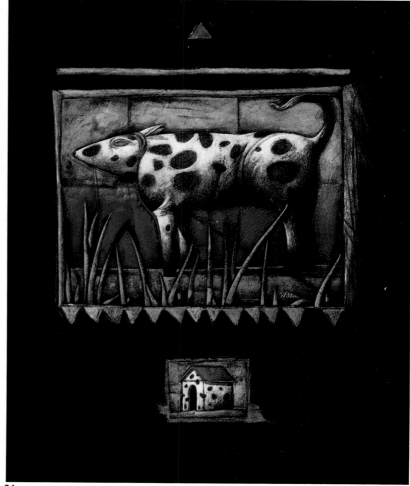

24

25

ARTIST: **MIKE HODGES**

ART DIRECTOR: Maryann B. Collins

CLIENT: Virginia Business Magazine

MEDIUM: Acrylic, Alkyds on Paper

SIZE: 20x16

26

ARTIST: **ROBERT HUNT**

ART DIRECTOR: Ed Guthero

CLIENT: Signs of the Times

MEDIUM: Oil on Canvas

SIZE: 18x23

27

ARTIST: **LINDA SCHARF**

ART DIRECTOR: Jill Winitzer

CLIENT: Lotus Magazine

MEDIUM: Pastel on Paper

SIZE: 14x12

28

ARTIST: **ROB DAY**

ART DIRECTOR: Patrick Coyne

CLIENT: Communication Arts

MEDIUM: Oil on Paper

SIZE: 12x10

25

26

27

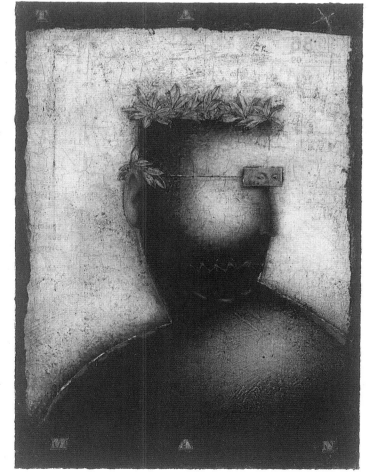

28

29

ARTIST: **JOHN LABBE**

ART DIRECTOR: Mark Shaw

CLIENT: East West

MEDIUM: Oil on Board

SIZE: 24x20

30

ARTIST: **JANET WOOLLEY**

ART DIRECTOR: Tim Gabor

CLIENT: New England Monthly

MEDIUM: Acrylic, Printed Images on Board

SIZE: 14x19

31

ARTIST: **WENDELL MINOR**

ART DIRECTOR: J. Porter

CLIENT: Yankee

MEDIUM: Acrylic on Masonite

SIZE: 24x18

32

ARTIST: **DANIEL CRAIG**

ART DIRECTOR: Susan McClelhan

CLIENT: Harrowsmith Country Life

MEDIUM: Acrylic on Board

SIZE: 25x21

29

30

31

32

33

ARTIST: **BRALDT BRALDS**

ART DIRECTOR: D.J. Stout, Fred Woodward

CLIENT: Texas Monthly

MEDIUM: Oil on Masonite

SIZE: 18x22

34

ARTIST: **PHILIP BURKE**

ART DIRECTOR: Patricia Bradbury, David Herbick

CLIENT: Newsweek

MEDIUM: Oil

SIZE: 36x148

35

ARTIST: **GREGORY MANCHESS**

ART DIRECTOR: Gary Gretter

CLIENT: Sports Afield

MEDIUM: Gouache

SIZE: 20x41

36

ARTIST: **GREGORY MANCHESS**

ART DIRECTOR: Paula Lehman

CLIENT: Cross & Crescent

MEDIUM: Oil

SIZE: 13x18

33

34

Lost poult
captured by
Cooper's Hawk...
discovered by sound...

35

36

37

ARTIST: **PETER DE SÈVE**

ART DIRECTOR: Robert Best

CLIENT: New York

MEDIUM: Watercolor, Ink on Watercolor Paper

SIZE: 12x9

38

ARTIST: **GARNET HENDERSON**

ART DIRECTOR: Robert Best

CLIENT: New York

MEDIUM: Watercolor

SIZE: 17x15

39

ARTIST: **GARNET HENDERSON**

ART DIRECTOR: Alex Gonzales

CLIENT: Gentlemen's Quarterly

MEDIUM: Watercolor

SIZE: 15x19

40

ARTIST: **ALAN BRUNETTIN**

ART DIRECTOR: Bob Fernandez

CLIENT: American Bar Association Journal

MEDIUM: Acrylic on Masonite, Clay Relief Sculpture

SIZE: 24x18

37

38

39

40

41

ARTIST: **TIM O'BRIEN**

ART DIRECTOR: Ken Palumbo

CLIENT: Playgirl Magazine

MEDIUM: Oil on Board

SIZE: 30x24

42

ARTIST: **KAM MAK**

ART DIRECTOR: Judy Garlan

CLIENT: The Atlantic Monthly

MEDIUM: Oil on Panel

SIZE: 20x26

43

ARTIST: **JOHN H. HOWARD**

ART DIRECTOR: Don DeMaio

CLIENT: The National Sports Daily

MEDIUM: Prisma Color on Black Paper

SIZE: 12x14

44

ARTIST: **DAVID POHL**

ART DIRECTOR: Michael Maskarinec

CLIENT: Pittsburgh Magazine

MEDIUM: Oil, Encaustic, Found Objects

SIZE: 32x25x5

42

43

44

45

ARTIST: **JOHN P. MAGGARD III**

ART DIRECTOR: Roy Behrens

CLIENT: The North American Review, University of Northern Iowa

MEDIUM: Acrylic, Oil on Board

SIZE: 30x20

46

ARTIST: **BILL FIRESTONE**

ART DIRECTOR: Richard Steadham, Peggy Robertson

CLIENT: Governing Magazine

MEDIUM: Acrylic on Board

SIZE: 11x12

47

ARTIST: **BETH BARTHOLOMEW**

ART DIRECTOR: Paul Davis

CLIENT: Wig Wag

MEDIUM: Casein on Board

SIZE: 12x10

48

ARTIST: **KAREN BARBOUR**

ART DIRECTOR: Robert Best

CLIENT: New York

MEDIUM: Gouache

SIZE: 22x18

45

46

47

48

49

ARTIST: **TIM O'BRIEN**

ART DIRECTOR: Tim O'Brien

MEDIUM: Oil on Board

SIZE: 24x18

50

ARTIST: **TED COCONIS**

ART DIRECTOR: Ted CoConis

CLIENT: Husberg Fine Art

MEDIUM: Oil on Canvas

SIZE: 30x40

51

ARTIST: **SCOTT REYNOLDS**

ART DIRECTOR: Ken Cendrowski

CLIENT: Corvette Quarterly

MEDIUM: Pastel, Oil

SIZE: 30x31

52

ARTIST: **SUSI KILGORE**

ART DIRECTOR: Tina Adamek

CLIENT: Senior Patient

MEDIUM: Oil on Paper

SIZE: 13x11

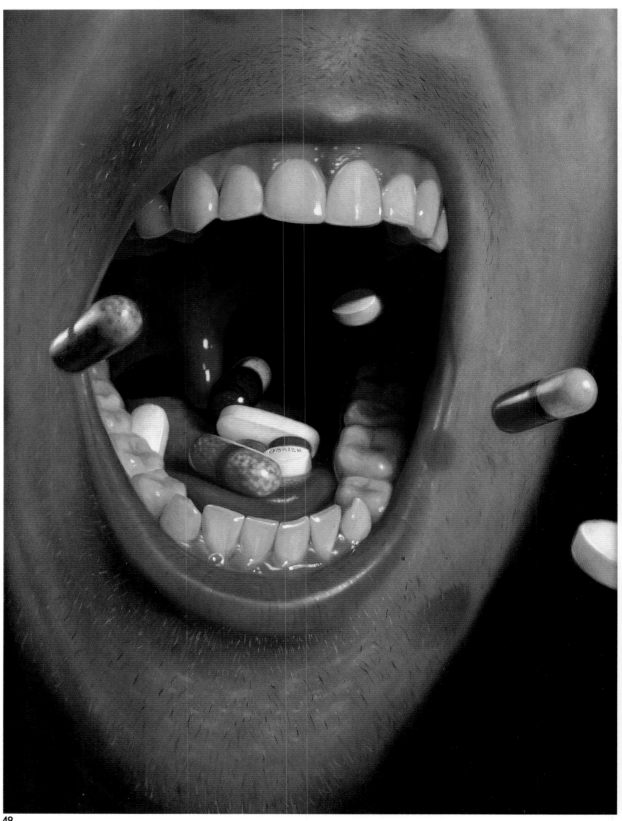

49

50

51

52

53

ARTIST: **FRED OTNES**

ART DIRECTOR: Yusaku Kamekura

CLIENT: Creation Magazine

MEDIUM: Collage, Oil, Acrylic on Linen

SIZE: 22x22

54

ARTIST: **TOM CURRY**

ART DIRECTOR: J. Porter

CLIENT: Yankee

MEDIUM: Acrylic Drybrush on Mylar

SIZE: 18x16

55

ARTIST: **FRED OTNES**

ART DIRECTOR: Yusaku Kamekura

CLIENT: Creation Magazine

MEDIUM: Collage, Oil, Acrylic on Linen

SIZE: 22x30

56

ARTIST: **GARY KELLEY**

ART DIRECTOR: Roy Behrens

CLIENT: The North American Review,
University of Northern Iowa

MEDIUM: Pastel on Paper

SIZE: 20x14

57

ARTIST: **ERIC DINYER**

ART DIRECTOR: Steven Powell, Jane Palecek

CLIENT: Hippocrates

MEDIUM: Oil on Paper

SIZE: 14x11

53

54

55

56

57

58

ARTIST: **RON LIGHTBURN**

ART DIRECTOR: Merwin Stewart

CLIENT: Listen Magazine

MEDIUM: Colored Pencil on Paper

SIZE: 30x25

59

ARTIST: **TOM CURRY**

ART DIRECTOR: Jane Palecek

CLIENT: In Health

MEDIUM: Acrylic Drybrush on Mylar

SIZE: 12x14

60

ARTIST: **GARY KELLEY**

ART DIRECTOR: Kent Barton

CLIENT: Sunshine Magazine

MEDIUM: Pastel, Cut Paper on Paper

SIZE: 22x22

61

ARTIST: **ERIC DINYER**

ART DIRECTOR: Chris Lotz

CLIENT: St. Louis Post Dispatch

MEDIUM: Oil on Paper

SIZE: 10x10

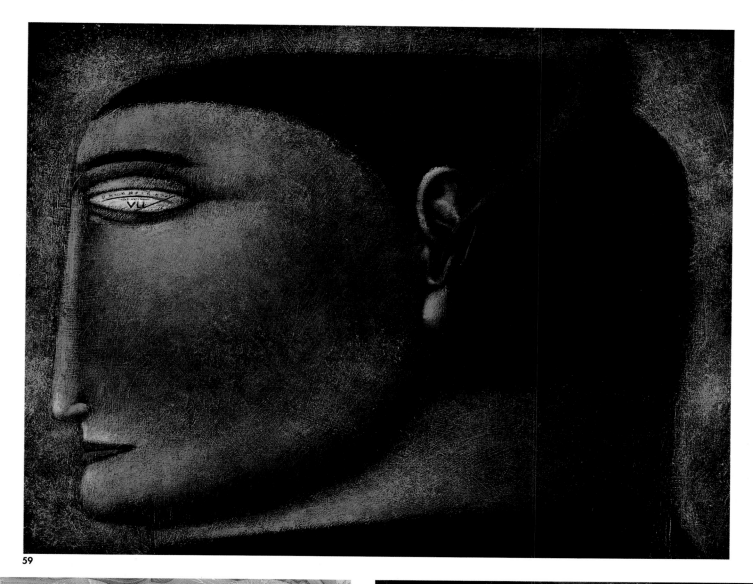

59

60

61

62

ARTIST: **W.C. BURGARD**

ART DIRECTOR: Kristen Lidke

CLIENT: Advance Magazine

MEDIUM: Oil Pastel on Paper

SIZE: 26x21

63

ARTIST: **JAMES SCOTT**

ART DIRECTOR: James Scott

MEDIUM: Acrylic, Oil on Canvas

SIZE: 16x20

64

ARTIST: **MATT MAHURIN**

ART DIRECTOR: George Karahastsos

CLIENT: The Globe & Mail

MEDIUM: Oil on Photograph

SIZE: 12x9

65

ARTIST: **EARL KELENY**

ART DIRECTOR: Naomi Trujillo

CLIENT: Discipleship Journal

MEDIUM: Oil

SIZE: 18x14

62

63

64

65

66

ARTIST: **WILLIAM LOW**

ART DIRECTOR: Norman Hotz

CLIENT: Reader's Digest

MEDIUM: Acrylic on Paper

SIZE: 28x28

67

ARTIST: **GREG SPALENKA**

ART DIRECTOR: Kerig Pope

CLIENT: Playboy

MEDIUM: Oil, Tape on Board

SIZE: 18x18

68

ARTIST: **HENRIK DRESCHER**

ART DIRECTOR: Jane Palecek

CLIENT: In Health

MEDIUM: Mixed Media

SIZE: 10x10

69

ARTIST: **ARTHUR SHILSTONE**

ART DIRECTOR: Caroline Despard

CLIENT: The Smithsonian

MEDIUM: Watercolor on Paper

SIZE: 21x26

66

67

68

69

70

ARTIST: **DON WELLER**

ART DIRECTOR: Richard M. Baron

CLIENT: Road & Track

MEDIUM: Watercolor, Dye, Pantone Plastic

SIZE: 20x16

71

ARTIST: **DEBRA WHITE**

ART DIRECTOR: Nancy Montgomery

CLIENT: Flowers &

MEDIUM: Oil, Collage on Watercolor Paper

SIZE: 19x14

72

ARTIST: **ALAN E. COBER**

ART DIRECTOR: Martha Geering

CLIENT: Sierra

MEDIUM: Ink, Watercolor, Prisma Color

SIZE: 18x14

73

ARTIST: **DUGALD STERMER**

ART DIRECTOR: Kimiko Horiike

CLIENT: Gulliver

MEDIUM: Watercolor, Pencil on Paper

SIZE: 24x18

74

ARTIST: **DUGALD STERMER**

ART DIRECTOR: Rosslyn Frick

CLIENT: New England Living

MEDIUM: Pencil, Watercolor on Paper

SIZE: 24x18

70

71

72

73

74

75

ARTIST: **WILSON McLEAN**

ART DIRECTOR: Kerig Pope

CLIENT: Playboy

MEDIUM: Oil on Canvas

SIZE: 20x20

76

ARTIST: **THEO RUDNAK**

ART DIRECTOR: Judy Garlan

CLIENT: The Atlantic Monthly

MEDIUM: Gouache

SIZE: 18x18

77

ARTIST: **BEN VERKAAIK**

ART DIRECTOR: Judy Garlan

CLIENT: The Atlantic Monthly

MEDIUM: Oil on Wood

SIZE: 30x34

78

ARTIST: **TIM JONKE**

ART DIRECTOR: Melissa Brown

CLIENT: Sun Magazine

MEDIUM: Oil on Board

SIZE: 18x18

79

ARTIST: **TIM JONKE**

ART DIRECTOR: Melissa Brown

CLIENT: Sun Magazine

MEDIUM: Oil on Board

SIZE: 18x18

75

76

77

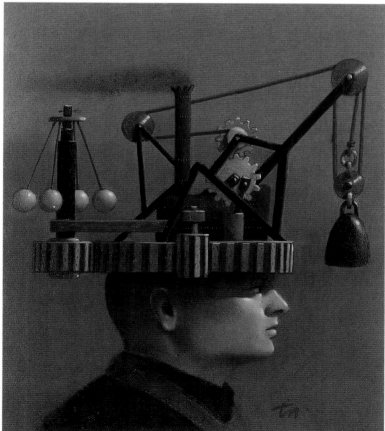

78

79

80

ARTIST: **CHRIS KIHLSTROM**

ART DIRECTOR: Chris Kihlstrom

MEDIUM: Silkscreen on Paper

SIZE: 27x21

81

ARTIST: **ROBERT G. STEELE**

ART DIRECTOR: Robert G. Steele

MEDIUM: Watercolor on Paper

SIZE: 9x11

82

ARTIST: **JUDY PEDERSEN**

ART DIRECTOR: J. Porter

CLIENT: Yankee

MEDIUM: Pastel on Pastel Cloth

SIZE: 14x13

83

ARTIST: **PETER FIORE**

ART DIRECTOR: Hector W. Marrero

CLIENT: Information Week

MEDIUM: Oil

SIZE: 24x18

80

81

82

83

84
ARTIST: **LAURA ALEXANDER**
ART DIRECTOR: Laura Alexander
MEDIUM: Oil on Canvas
SIZE: 21x17

85
ARTIST: **ROBERT G. STEELE**
ART DIRECTOR: J. Porter
CLIENT: Yankee
MEDIUM: Watercolor on Watercolor Paper
SIZE: 8x13

86
ARTIST: **PAUL ROGERS**
ART DIRECTOR: Dave Willardson
CLIENT: L.A.X. Magazine
MEDIUM: Acrylic, Ink, Matrocolor on Board
SIZE: 20x16

87
ARTIST: **WILLIAM LOW**
ART DIRECTOR: William Low
MEDIUM: Oil on Paper
SIZE: 30x22

84

85

86

87

88

ARTIST: **TIM JESSELL**

ART DIRECTOR: Hector W. Marrero

CLIENT: Information Week

MEDIUM: Pastel, Colored Pencils on Paper

SIZE: 20x20

89

ARTIST: **CARTER GOODRICH**

ART DIRECTOR: Lois Erlacher

CLIENT: Emergency Medicine

MEDIUM: Colored Pencil on Watercolor Paper

SIZE: 15x24

90

ARTIST: **DANIEL SCHWARTZ**

ART DIRECTOR: Daniel Schwartz

MEDIUM: Oil on Paper

SIZE: 30x23

91

ARTIST: **SAM WARD**

ART DIRECTOR: Bob Fernandez

CLIENT: American Bar Association Journal

MEDIUM: Gouache on Board

SIZE: 28x22

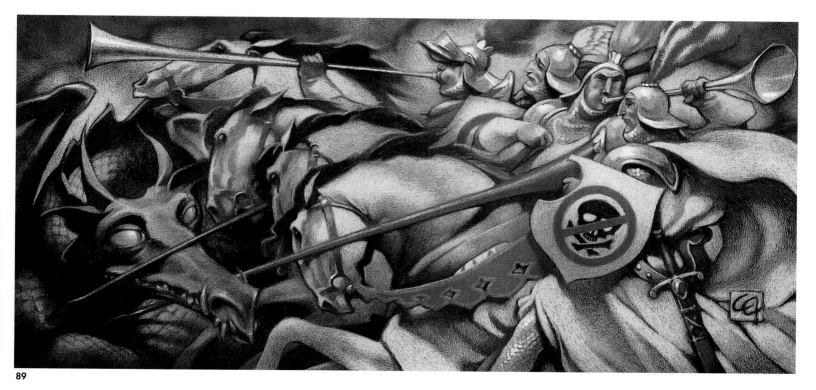

89

90

91

92

ARTIST: **HIROKO**

ART DIRECTOR: Alma Phipps

CLIENT: Chief Executive

MEDIUM: Acrylic on Linen

SIZE: 20x16

93

ARTIST: **MARK ENGLISH**

ART DIRECTOR: Mark English

MEDIUM: Oil

SIZE: 41x56

94

ARTIST: **JOHN RUSH**

ART DIRECTOR: Dianne Gibson

CLIENT: American Way Magazine

MEDIUM: Gouache, Acrylic on Linen Board

SIZE: 28x22

95

ARTIST: **GLENN HARRINGTON**

ART DIRECTOR: Jana Khalifa

CLIENT: Playgirl Magazine

MEDIUM: Oil on Board

SIZE: 27x24

92

93

94

95

96

ARTIST: **PAUL ROGERS**

ART DIRECTOR: Rikki Poulos

CLIENT: Playboy Jazz Festival

MEDIUM: Acrylic, Ink, Matrocolor on Board

SIZE: 18x14

97

ARTIST: **STEVE JOHNSON**

ART DIRECTOR: Lisa Michurski

CLIENT: Newsweek

MEDIUM: Oil on Watercolor Paper

SIZE: 14x18

98

ARTIST: **STEVE BRODNER**

ART DIRECTOR: Michael Grossman, Miriam Campiz

CLIENT: Entertainment Weekly

MEDIUM: Acrylic on Scratchboard

SIZE: 20x15

99

ARTIST: **STEVE BRODNER**

ART DIRECTOR: Barbara Richer

CLIENT: The New York Times Magazine

MEDIUM: Acrylic on Scratchboard

SIZE: 20x15

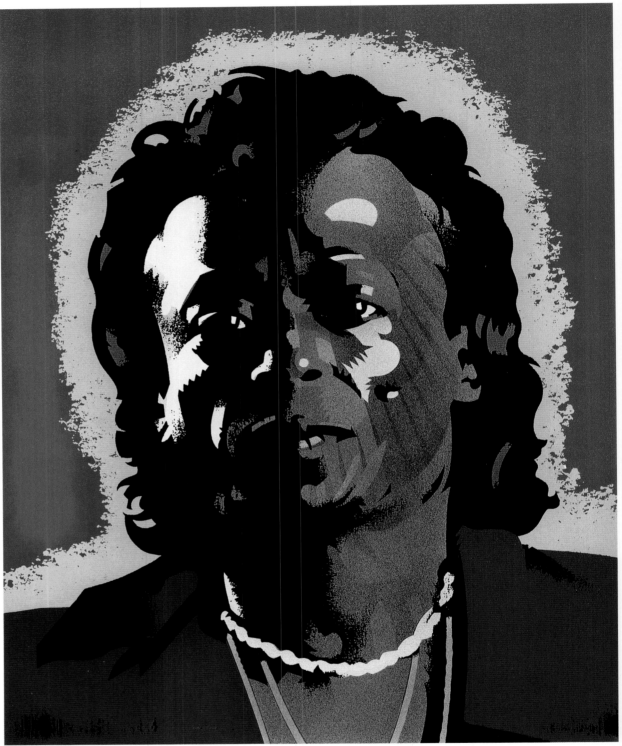

96

97

98

99

100

ARTIST: **LAURA SMITH**

ART DIRECTOR: Richard Mantel

CLIENT: New York

MEDIUM: Gouache

SIZE: 13X10

101

ARTIST: **BRAD HOLLAND**

ART DIRECTOR: Hans Georg Pospischl

CLIENT: Frankfurter Allgemeine Magazine

MEDIUM: Acrylic on Masonite

SIZE: 19x25

102

ARTIST: **BRAD HOLLAND**

ART DIRECTOR: Richard Bleiweiss

CLIENT: Penthouse Letters

MEDIUM: Acrylic on Masonite

SIZE: 24x18

103

ARTIST: **DOUGLAS ANDELIN**

ART DIRECTOR: Melissa Wasserman

CLIENT: Spin Magazine

MEDIUM: Pastel, Watercolor

SIZE: 24x18

100

101

102

103

104

ARTIST: **DAVID SHANNON**

ART DIRECTOR: Mare Earley

CLIENT: Chicago Tribune Magazine

MEDIUM: Acrylic on Board

SIZE: 24x18

105

ARTIST: **JAMES McMULLAN**

ART DIRECTOR: Carol Carson

CLIENT: Scholastic Magazine

MEDIUM: Watercolor on Paper

SIZE: 23x32

106

ARTIST: **JAMES McMULLAN**

ART DIRECTOR: Robert Best

CLIENT: New York

MEDIUM: Watercolor on Paper

SIZE: 17x14

107

ARTIST: **JOSÉ ORTEGA**

ART DIRECTOR: Paul Davis

CLIENT: Wig Wag

MEDIUM: Scratchboard, Photocopy, Ink, Marker

SIZE: 13x10

104

105

106

107

108

ARTIST: **CARY HENRIE**

ART DIRECTOR: Joy Toltzis Makon, Deborah Dinger

CLIENT: Voice Magazine

MEDIUM: Oil on Paper

SIZE: 16x13

109

ARTIST: **JANET WOOLLEY**

ART DIRECTOR: Andrea Burns

CLIENT: Special Report

MEDIUM: Collage, Acrylic on Board

SIZE: 20x30

110

ARTIST: **GREG SPALENKA**

ART DIRECTOR: Kitty McGee

CLIENT: AZ Magazine

MEDIUM: Collage, Paint, Tape, Shellac

SIZE: 20x18

111

ARTIST: **GREG SPALENKA**

ART DIRECTOR: Steve Hoffmann

CLIENT: Sports Illustrated

MEDIUM: Collage, Paint, Tape on Board

SIZE: 15x10

108

109

110

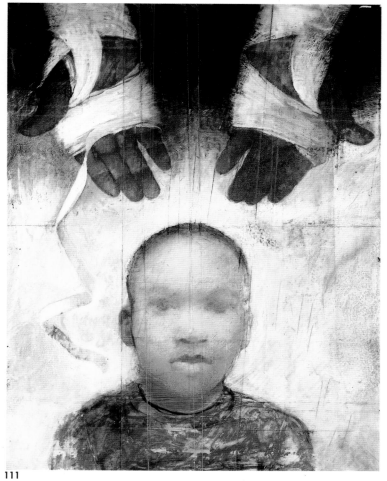

111

112

ARTIST: **MERRITT DEKLE**

ART DIRECTOR: Greg Klee

CLIENT: Boston Magazine

MEDIUM: Acrylic on Board

SIZE: 20x15

113

ARTIST: **RICHARD HULL**

ART DIRECTOR: Nickie Egan

CLIENT: WordPerfect Magazine

MEDIUM: Acrylic

SIZE: 20x30

114

ARTIST: **ROBERT HUNT**

ART DIRECTOR: Robert Hunt

CLIENT: Communication Arts

MEDIUM: Oil on Paper

SIZE: 30x26

115

ARTIST: **SKIP LIEPKE**

ART DIRECTOR: Skip Liepke

MEDIUM: Oil

SIZE: 10x8

112

113

114

115

116
ARTIST: **C.F. PAYNE**
ART DIRECTOR: Fred Woodward
CLIENT: Rolling Stone
MEDIUM: Mixed Media
SIZE: 15x14

117
ARTIST: **JOHN D. DAWSON**
ART DIRECTOR: Howard Paine
CLIENT: National Geographic
MEDIUM: Mixed Media
SIZE: 18x24

118
ARTIST: **C.F. PAYNE**
ART DIRECTOR: Fred Woodward
CLIENT: Rolling Stone
MEDIUM: Mixed Media
SIZE: 15x14

119
ARTIST: **C.F. PAYNE**
ART DIRECTOR: Janet Froelich
CLIENT: The New York Times Magazine
MEDIUM: Mixed Media
SIZE: 17x15

116

117

118

119

BOOK JURY

Keith Ferris
CHAIRMAN, AVIATION ARTIST

Braldt Bralds
ILLUSTRATOR

Ida Libby Dengrove
ILLUSTRATOR

Vivienne Flesher
ILLUSTRATOR

Al Karsten
PROMOTION ART DIRECTOR
THE NEW YORK TIMES

Forbes Lloyd Linkhorn
ART DIRECTOR

Marvin Mattelson
ILLUSTRATOR

Jacqui Morgan
ILLUSTRATOR, PAINTER, AUTHOR

Carol Wald
ILLUSTRATOR: PAINTINGS & COLLAGE

AWARD WINNERS

Michael J. Deas
GOLD MEDAL

———

Carter Goodrich
GOLD MEDAL

———

Bert Kitchen
GOLD MEDAL

———

Merritt Dekle
SILVER MEDAL

———

Stasys Eidrigevicius
SILVER MEDAL

———

William Low
SILVER MEDAL

B
O
O
K

CARTER GOODRICH

"Born in Washington, DC, in 1959; graduated from Rhode Island School of Design in 1981. Dabbled in political cartooning and stunk up the joint; moved to New York in 1983 and began my career as a professional illustrator. Some of my clients include *Playboy, GQ, Forbes, Time, Newsweek, Connoisseur,* Bantam, Grove, Macmillan, various advertising agencies, and an illustrated edition of the "Nutcracker" for Knopf."

120

ARTIST: **CARTER GOODRICH**

ART DIRECTOR: Krystyna Skalski

CLIENT: Grove Weidenfeld

MEDIUM: Colored Pencil on Watercolor Paper

SIZE: 23x18

121

ARTIST: **MICHAEL J. DEAS**

ART DIRECTOR: Ellen Friedman

CLIENT: William Morrow & Co., Inc.

MEDIUM: Oil on Panel

SIZE: 26x20

BERT KITCHEN

"I have spent the majority of my life so far as a painter, although in the last ten years I have produced six children's books as the author and illustrator. I have found this to be a happy combination which creates a very good balance, with no conflict or compromise involved whatsoever."

122

ARTIST: **BERT KITCHEN**

ART DIRECTOR: Atha Tehon

CLIENT: Dial Books for Young Readers

MEDIUM: Watercolor, Gouache, Colored Pencil

SIZE: 12x15

STASYS EIDRIGEVICIUS

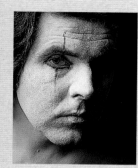

"I was born in the north of Lithuania. My art school was in Kaunas and Art Akademy in Vilnius. In 1980 I moved to Warsaw and now I have visited USA, Japan, and many countries in Europe with my exhibitions or to receive awards for my posters, children's book illustrations, etc. My most successful exhibition was in Roma in 1991, at the gallery Specchi dell`Ert. When I see stone, wood, paper, metal—it's inspiration for my work—and life. When I'm traveling I make many sketches...I think it's very important to be with creation all the time, during day and night."

123

ARTIST: **STASYS EIDRIGEVICIUS**

ART DIRECTOR: Brigitte Sidjanski, Kati Korpijaakko

CLIENT: North-South Books

MEDIUM: Pastel, Gouache

SIZE: 18x16

"It took a long time to come up with this scene for the book, *A Woman's Glory*, because all of my sketches were rejected by the editors. It got to the point where I was getting concerned about finishing the illustration in time since I was planning to go to Cape Cod. Unfortunately, I was unable to get an approved sketch, so I took my work with me on my vacation. It really wasn't too bad, though, because the idea I came up with came from a sketch I made of an old gas station I saw near Truro on Cape Cod. It was perfect for the book and I had a lot of fun doing it..."

124

ARTIST: **WILLIAM LOW**

ART DIRECTOR: Joseph Montebello

CLIENT: HarperCollins Publishers

MEDIUM: Acrylic on Paper

SIZE: 20x17

MERRITT DEKLE

"A Southern Gothic childhood and a N.Y.C. adulthood have given me a reverie for the past, an intolerance of the present, and a dread of the future. I have taken my angst, my fax machine, and my faith in Federal Express and returned to my roots where I face my destiny as a Southern eccentric."

125

ARTIST: **MERRITT DEKLE**

ART DIRECTOR: Neil Stuart

CLIENT: Dutton Books

MEDIUM: Acrylic on Board

SIZE: 14x11

126

ARTIST: **JERRY LOFARO**

ART DIRECTOR: Peter Kruzan

CLIENT: Doubleday

MEDIUM: Acrylic on Paper

SIZE: 14x20

127

ARTIST: **JAMES WARHOLA**

ART DIRECTOR: Diane Luger

CLIENT: Berkley Publishing

MEDIUM: Oil

SIZE: 30x40

128

ARTIST: **GREGORY MANCHESS**

ART DIRECTOR: Gregory Manchess

CLIENT: Dark Harvest Press

MEDIUM: Oil

SIZE: 16X29

129

ARTIST: **BETSY GOSHEFF SCIBLE**

ART DIRECTOR: Betsy Gosheff Scible

MEDIUM: Oil

SIZE: 20x17

130

ARTIST: **CHRISTINE RODIN**

ART DIRECTOR: Marietta Anastassatos

CLIENT: Dell Publishing

MEDIUM: Mixed Media

SIZE: 13x10

126

127

128

129

130

131

ARTIST: **MICHAEL GARLAND**

ART DIRECTOR: Gianella Garrett

CLIENT: Chelsea House

MEDIUM: Oil on Watercolor Paper

SIZE: 26x23

132

ARTIST: **MARK BUEHNER**

ART DIRECTOR: Atha Tehon

CLIENT: Dial Books for Young Readers

MEDIUM: Oil, Acrylics on Board

SIZE: 14x17

133

ARTIST: **MARK SUMMERS**

ART DIRECTOR: Sara Eisenman

CLIENT: Houghton Mifflin

MEDIUM: Scratchboard, Ink

SIZE: 12x9

134

ARTIST: **JOHN MARTINEZ**

ART DIRECTOR: Jackie Merri Meyer

CLIENT: Warner Books

MEDIUM: Pen and Ink, Process Color

SIZE: 8x6

131

132

133

134

135
ARTIST: **CATHLEEN TOELKE**
ART DIRECTOR: Joseph Montebello
CLIENT: HarperCollins Publishers
MEDIUM: Gouache on Watercolor Board
SIZE: 21x18

136
ARTIST: **JOHN RUSH**
ART DIRECTOR: Carol Carson
CLIENT: Alfred A. Knopf
MEDIUM: Gouache on Linen Board
SIZE: 28x38

137
ARTIST: **DUGALD STERMER**
ART DIRECTOR: Gina Davis
CLIENT: Pantheon Books
MEDIUM: Pencil, Watercolor on Paper
SIZE: 24x18

138
ARTIST: **ETIENNE DELESSERT**
ART DIRECTOR: Rita Marshall
CLIENT: Stewart, Tabori & Chang
MEDIUM: Watercolor, Pencil
SIZE: 14x12

135

136

137

138

139
ARTIST: **STEVE JOHNSON**
ART DIRECTOR: Mary Sailer
CLIENT: William C. Brown Publishers
MEDIUM: Oil on Watercolor Paper
SIZE: 17x17

140
ARTIST: **ELWOOD H. SMITH**
ART DIRECTOR: Mary Ellen Podgorski
CLIENT: Klutz Press
MEDIUM: Watercolor, Ink
SIZE: 14x14

141
ARTIST: **HERBERT TAUSS**
ART DIRECTOR: Herbert Tauss
MEDIUM: Charcoal on Canvas
SIZE: 42x48

142
ARTIST: **HERBERT TAUSS**
ART DIRECTOR: Herbert Tauss
MEDIUM: Charcoal on Canvas
SIZE: 36x48

143
ARTIST: **KAY WELLEN GONTAREK**
ART DIRECTOR: Kay Wellen Gontarek
MEDIUM: Pencil, Watercolor on Board
SIZE: 15x20

139

140

141

142

143

144

ARTIST: **ROBERTO INNOCENTI**

ART DIRECTOR: Rita Marshall

CLIENT: Stewart, Tabori & Chang

MEDIUM: Watercolor

SIZE: 12x9

145

ARTIST: **BRENT WHITE**

ART DIRECTOR: Brent White

MEDIUM: Oil

SIZE: 36x78

146

ARTIST: **PHILLIP SINGER**

ART DIRECTOR: Jackie Merri Meyer

CLIENT: Warner Books

MEDIUM: Acrylic

SIZE: 12x8

147

ARTIST: **PHILLIP SINGER**

ART DIRECTOR: Jackie Merri Meyer

CLIENT: Warner Books

MEDIUM: Acrylic

SIZE: 12x8

144

145

146

147

148

ARTIST: **BRALDT BRALDS**

ART DIRECTOR: Betsy Wollheim

CLIENT: Daw Books

MEDIUM: Oil on Paper

SIZE: 18x14

149

ARTIST: **WALTER RANE**

ART DIRECTOR: Georgia Morrissey

CLIENT: Scholastic, Inc.

MEDIUM: Oil on Board

SIZE: 15x20

150

ARTIST: **KINUKO Y. CRAFT**

ART DIRECTOR: Wendy Bass

CLIENT: Atheneum

MEDIUM: Gouache on Board

SIZE: 21x10

151

ARTIST: **JAMES SKISTIMAS**

ART DIRECTOR: James Skistimas

MEDIUM: Oil, Gouache, Acrylic

SIZE: 27x22

149

150

151

152

ARTIST: **RUTH SANDERSON**

ART DIRECTOR: Susan Lu

CLIENT: Little, Brown & Co.

MEDIUM: Oil on Canvas

SIZE: 24x36

153

ARTIST: **CHRISTOPHER WORMELL**

ART DIRECTOR: Atha Tehon

CLIENT: Dial Books for Young Readers

MEDIUM: Linoleum Print on Paper

SIZE: 11x11

154

ARTIST: **JIM BURNS**

ART DIRECTOR: Jamie Warren

CLIENT: Bantam Books

MEDIUM: Oil on Canvas

SIZE: 20x45

155

ARTIST: **ALAN E. COBER**

ART DIRECTOR: Wendy Bass

CLIENT: Macmillan Publishing Co.

MEDIUM: Watercolor, Ink

SIZE: 12x11

156

ARTIST: **DAVID STIMSON**

ART DIRECTOR: Victor Weaver

CLIENT: Dell Publishing

MEDIUM: Acrylic on Canvas

SIZE: 18x12

152

153

154

155

156

157

ARTIST: **CHRIS GALL**

ART DIRECTOR: Neil Stuart

CLIENT: Viking Books

MEDIUM: Scratchboard

SIZE: 16x8

158

ARTIST: **JERRY LOFARO**

ART DIRECTOR: Peter Kruzan

CLIENT: Doubleday

MEDIUM: Acrylic on Watercolor Paper

SIZE: 14x20

159

ARTIST: **CARTER GOODRICH**

ART DIRECTOR: Jamie Warren Youll

CLIENT: Bantam Books

MEDIUM: Colored Pencil on Watercolor Paper

SIZE: 21x16

160

ARTIST: **KENT WILLIAMS**

ART DIRECTOR: Karen Berger

CLIENT: DC Comics

MEDIUM: Mixed Media on Paper

SIZE: 20x16

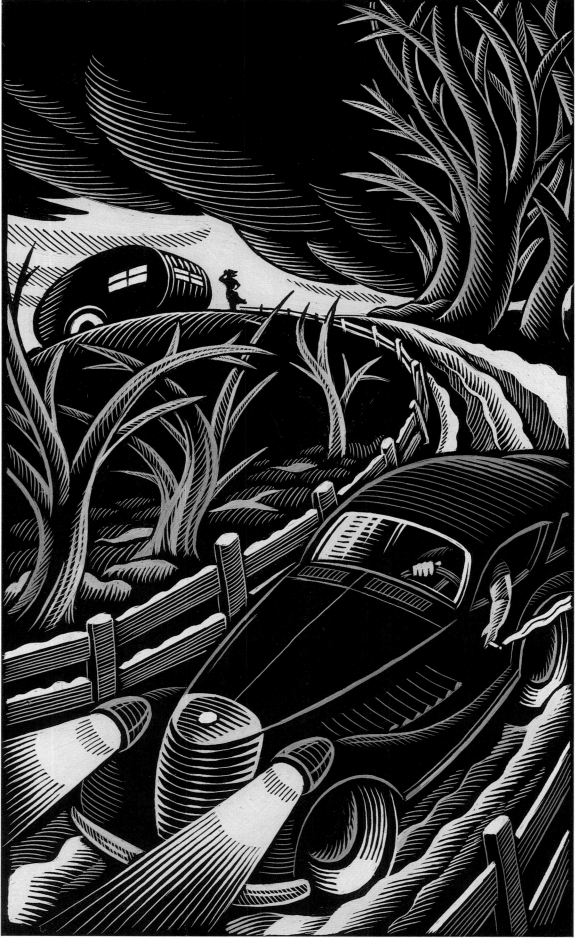

158

159

160

161

ARTIST: **DEBRA WHITE**

ART DIRECTOR: Melissa Jacoby

CLIENT: Penguin USA

MEDIUM: Oil and Collage

SIZE: 20x16

162

ARTIST: **JERRY PINKNEY**

ART DIRECTOR: Atha Tehon

CLIENT: Dial Books for Young Readers

MEDIUM: Pencil, Watercolor on Paper

SIZE: 15x17

163

ARTIST: **KENT WILLIAMS**

ART DIRECTOR: Dan Chichester

CLIENT: Epic Comics

MEDIUM: Watercolor

SIZE: 23x15

164

ARTIST: **KENT WILLIAMS**

ART DIRECTOR: Marc McLaurin

CLIENT: Epic Comics

MEDIUM: Collage and Oil

SIZE: 17x12

161

162

163

164

165

ARTIST: **MELISSA GRIMES**

ART DIRECTOR: Steve Eanes

CLIENT: Navigators Press

MEDIUM: Laser Copy Collage on Boar

SIZE: 25x25

166

ARTIST: **JOHN THOMPSON**

ART DIRECTOR: Robert Grant

CLIENT: Reader's Digest

MEDIUM: Acrylic on Board

SIZE: 26x40

167

ARTIST: **TED RAND**

ART DIRECTOR: Golda Lauren

CLIENT: G.P. Putnam's Sons

MEDIUM: Watercolor

SIZE: 20x28

168

ARTIST: **JEFF MEYER**

ART DIRECTOR: Jeff Meyer

MEDIUM: Linoleum Cut over Acrylic

SIZE: 17x15

169

ARTIST: **ROBERT GOLDSTROM**

ART DIRECTOR: Wendy Bass

CLIENT: Scribners

MEDIUM: Oil on Canvas

SIZE: 17x15

165

166

167

168

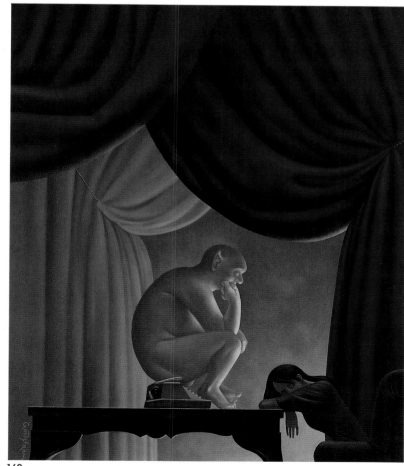

169

170

ARTIST: **BILL SIENKIEWICZ**

ART DIRECTOR: Wade Roberts, Alex Wald

CLIENT: Berkley/First Publishing

MEDIUM: Mixed Media

SIZE: 34x24

171

ARTIST: **WILSON McLEAN**

ART DIRECTOR: Frank Metz

CLIENT: Poseidon Press

MEDIUM: Oil on Canvas

SIZE: 20x30

172

ARTIST: **DAVID SHANNON**

ART DIRECTOR: Gina Davis

CLIENT: Pantheon Books

MEDIUM: Acrylic on Board

SIZE: 18x12

173

ARTIST: **CHRIS McALLISTER**

ART DIRECTOR: Leslie Osher

CLIENT: Simon & Schuster

MEDIUM: Acrylic on Board

SIZE: 17x15

171

172

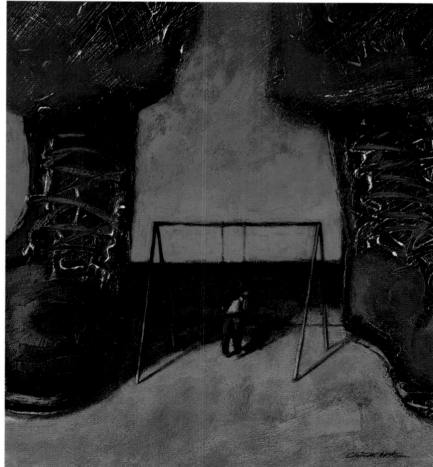

173

174

ARTIST: **TOM SCIACCA**

ART DIRECTOR: Jim Plumeri

CLIENT: Bantam Books

MEDIUM: Acrylic on Board

SIZE: 7x5

175

ARTIST: **JIM BURNS**

ART DIRECTOR: Marietta Anastassatos

CLIENT: Dell Publishing

MEDIUM: Oil on Canvas

SIZE: 24x36

176

ARTIST: **JOANIE SCHWARTZ**

ART DIRECTOR: George Cornell

CLIENT: New American Library

MEDIUM: Oil on Photograph

SIZE: 14x11

177

ARTIST: **JENNY TYLDEN-WRIGHT**

ART DIRECTOR: Neil Stuart

CLIENT: Viking Books

MEDIUM: Colored Pencils on Board

SIZE: 24x18

175

176

177

178

ARTIST: **CAROL INOUYE**

ART DIRECTOR: Christine Van Bree

CLIENT: Scribners

MEDIUM: Watercolor

SIZE: 13x14

179

ARTIST: **BETH PECK**

ART DIRECTOR: Denise Cronin

CLIENT: Alfred A. Knopf

MEDIUM: Watercolor, Pen, Ink on Paper

SIZE: 18x15

180

ARTIST: **JIM WARREN**

ART DIRECTOR: Jamie Warren

CLIENT: Bantam Books

MEDIUM: Oil on Canvas

SIZE: 20x20

181

ARTIST: **DIANA ZELVIN**

ART DIRECTOR: Lee Ann Martin

MEDIUM: Oil on Board

SIZE: 12x15

182

ARTIST: **BRIAN AJHAR**

ART DIRECTOR: Patti Eslinger

CLIENT: Washington Square Press

MEDIUM: Watercolor, Ink, Prisma Color

SIZE: 28x20

178

179

180

181

182

183

ARTIST: **ED RENFRO**

ART DIRECTOR: Ed Renfro

CLIENT: Jeffrey Publishing

MEDIUM: Pen, Ink, Dyes on Paper

SIZE: 26x21

184

ARTIST: **ROY PENDLETON**

ART DIRECTOR: Roy Pendleton

MEDIUM: Acrylics on Canvas

SIZE: 15x22

185

ARTIST: **WILLIAM LOW**

ART DIRECTOR: Joan O'Conner

CLIENT: McGraw Hill Publishers

MEDIUM: Oil on Paper

SIZE: 30x22

186

ARTIST: **CHARLES MIKOLAYCAK**

ART DIRECTOR: David Rogers

CLIENT: Holiday House, Inc.

MEDIUM: Watercolor, Colored Pencil on Print

SIZE: 13x10

183

184

185

186

187

ARTIST: **GARY KELLEY**

ART DIRECTOR: Rita Marshall

CLIENT: Creative Education/Stewart, Tabori & Chang

MEDIUM: Pastel on Paper

SIZE: 20x12

188

ARTIST: **JERRY PINKNEY**

ART DIRECTOR: Cecilia Yung

CLIENT: Macmillan Publishing Co.

MEDIUM: Pencil, Watercolor on Paper

SIZE: 17x23

189

ARTIST: **SUSI KILGORE**

ART DIRECTOR: Frank Metz

CLIENT: Simon & Schuster

MEDIUM: Oil on Board

SIZE: 20x16

190

ARTIST: **SEAN P. LYNCH**

ART DIRECTOR: Sean P. Lynch

MEDIUM: Oil on Board

SIZE: 25x20

187

188

189

190

191

ARTIST: **MICHAEL CHRISTMAN**

ART DIRECTOR: Krystyna Skalski

CLIENT: Grove Weidenfeld

MEDIUM: Acrylic, Oil, Pencil

SIZE: 16x16

192

ARTIST: **JEFF MEYER**

ART DIRECTOR: Jeff Meyer

MEDIUM: Pastel, Acrylic, Charcoal, Pencils

SIZE: 44x46

193

ARTIST: **WALTER RANE**

ART DIRECTOR: Soren Noring

CLIENT: Reader's Digest

MEDIUM: Oil on Board

SIZE: 24x36

194

ARTIST: **ADAM NICKLEWICZ**

ART DIRECTOR: Melissa Jacoby

CLIENT: Plume Books

MEDIUM: Oil

SIZE: 10x8

195

ARTIST: **MEL ODOM**

ART DIRECTOR: Steven Brower

CLIENT: Carol Publishing

MEDIUM: Collage on Board

SIZE: 14x11

191

192

193

194

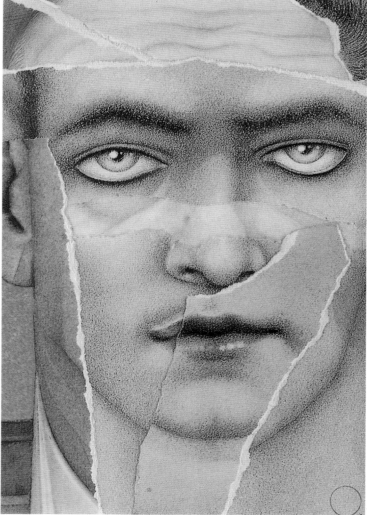

195

196

ARTIST: **THOMAS CANTY**

ART DIRECTOR: Judy Murello

CLIENT: Penguin USA

MEDIUM: Oil on Paper

SIZE: 33x22

197

ARTIST: **PETER FIORE**

ART DIRECTOR: Al Giunta

CLIENT: Memorial Hospital

MEDIUM: Oil

SIZE: 15x26

198

ARTIST: **PETER FIORE**

ART DIRECTOR: Don Munson

CLIENT: Random House

MEDIUM: Oil

SIZE: 22x15

199

ARTIST: **PETER FIORE**

ART DIRECTOR: Susan Newman

CLIENT: Paragon House

MEDIUM: Oil

SIZE: 24x18

197

198

199

200

ARTIST: **MARK HESS**

ART DIRECTOR: Jackie Merri Meyer

CLIENT: Warner Books

MEDIUM: Acrylic

SIZE: 18x12

201

ARTIST: **BETH PECK**

ART DIRECTOR: Lucia Monfried

CLIENT: E.P. Dutton

MEDIUM: Oil on Watercolor Paper

SIZE: 12x19

202

ARTIST: **MERRITT DEKLE**

ART DIRECTOR: Morris Taub

CLIENT: New American Library

MEDIUM: Acrylic on Board

SIZE: 22x15

203

ARTIST: **MERRITT DEKLE**

ART DIRECTOR: Tom Egner

CLIENT: Avon Books

MEDIUM: Acrylic on Board

SIZE: 20x14

200

201

202

203

204

ARTIST: **PATRICIA ROHRBACHER**

ART DIRECTOR: Patricia Rohrbacher

MEDIUM: Oil on Canvas

SIZE: 24x20

205

ARTIST: **J.K. POTTER**

ART DIRECTOR: Jamie Warren Youll

CLIENT: Bantam Books

MEDIUM: Handcolored Photo Collage

SIZE: 20x24

206

ARTIST: **DAVID SHANNON**

ART DIRECTOR: Susan Newman

CLIENT: Paragon House

MEDIUM: Acrylic on Board

SIZE: 18x12

207

ARTIST: **MEL ODOM**

ART DIRECTOR: Jackie Merri Meyer

CLIENT: Warner Books/Mysterious Press

MEDIUM: Dye, Gouache, Pencil

SIZE: 12x9

204

205

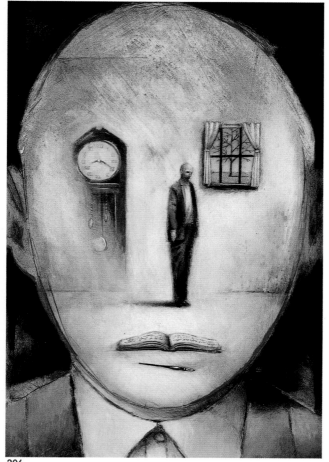

206

207

208

ARTIST: **NIKOLAI PUNIN**

ART DIRECTOR: Krystyna Skalski

CLIENT: Grove Weidenfeld

SIZE: 16x18

209

ARTIST: **LOIS EHLERT**

ART DIRECTOR: Michael Farmer

CLIENT: Harcourt Brace Javanovich

MEDIUM: Watercolor, Collage on Paper

SIZE: 18x20

210

ARTIST: **SKIP LIEPKE**

ART DIRECTOR: Skip Liepke

MEDIUM: Oil

SIZE: 28x42

211

ARTIST: **MARK ENGLISH**

ART DIRECTOR: Mark English

MEDIUM: Oil

SIZE: 42x30

212

ARTIST: **SKIP LIEPKE**

ART DIRECTOR: Skip Liepke

MEDIUM: Oil

SIZE: 26x24

208

209

210

211

212

213

ARTIST: **BOB CROFUT**

ART DIRECTOR: Tom Egner

CLIENT: Avon Books

MEDIUM: Oil, Ink on Muslin

SIZE: 28x20

214

ARTIST: **ED LINDLOF**

ART DIRECTOR: Neil Stuart

CLIENT: Dutton Books

MEDIUM: Acrylic

SIZE: 24x36

215

ARTIST: **CAROL WALD**

ART DIRECTOR: Babette Cabral, Denise Gouelette

CLIENT: The National Watercolor Society

MEDIUM: Watercolor

SIZE: 12x12

216

ARTIST: **JERRY PINKNEY**

ART DIRECTOR: Cecilia Yung

CLIENT: Macmillan Publishing Co.

MEDIUM: Pencil, Watercolor on Paper

SIZE: 17x14

213

214

215

216

217

ARTIST: **C. MICHAEL DUDASH**
ART DIRECTOR: Gerry Counihan
CLIENT: Dell/Delacorte Press
MEDIUM: Oil on Linen on Board
SIZE: 28x19

218

ARTIST: **WILLIAM JOYCE**
ART DIRECTOR: Harriett Barton, Christine Kettner
CLIENT: HarperCollins Publishers
MEDIUM: Acrylic on Watercolor Paper
SIZE: 23x30

219

ARTIST: **JOHN NICKLE**
ART DIRECTOR: Jim Davis
CLIENT: Crown Publishing
MEDIUM: Colored Pencil on Black Paper
SIZE: 17x14

220

ARTIST: **JOHN NICKLE**
CLIENT: Henry Holt Juvenile Books
MEDIUM: Colored Pencil on Gray Paper
SIZE: 17x14

217

218

219

220

221
ARTIST: **ROBERT CRAWFORD**
ART DIRECTOR: Joseph Montebello
CLIENT: HarperCollins Publishers
MEDIUM: Acrylic on Canvas
SIZE: 27x21

222
ARTIST: **ERIC FOWLER**
ART DIRECTOR: Melissa Jacoby
CLIENT: Penguin Books
MEDIUM: Oil on Paper
SIZE: 18x24

223
ARTIST: **HARRY F. BLISS**
MEDIUM: Watercolor on Paper
SIZE: 18x14

224
ARTIST: **GARY HEAD**
ART DIRECTOR: Gary Head
MEDIUM: Oil on Canvas
SIZE: 12x8

222

223

224

ADVERTISING JURY

Bob Cuevas
CHAIRMAN, GRAPHIC ILLUSTRATOR & DESIGNER

Paul Calle
PAINTER, STAMP DESIGNER, AUTHOR

Art Cumings
HUMOROUS & SATIRICAL ILLUSTRATOR

Etienne Delessert
ILLUSTRATOR

Susan Newman
ART DIRECTOR, PARAGON HOUSE

C.F. Payne
ILLUSTRATOR

Charles Reid
ILLUSTRATOR

John Rush
ILLUSTRATOR

Tamara Schneider
CREATIVE DIRECTOR, *LADIES' HOME JOURNAL*

AWARD WINNERS

Brad Holland
GOLD MEDAL

———————

Fred Otnes
SILVER MEDAL

———————

Janet Woolley
SILVER MEDAL

ADVERTISING

"This is a totally meaningless picture and it becomes more meaningless every time I comment on it. At first I was surprised, finally I was baffled at how many people think it's a woman dancing with Mickey Mouse. When Americans can't tell Mickey Mouse from a cheesy alley cat any longer I'm at a loss for words.

"The picture came about because I was stranded in San Diego with a large box of crayolas and this seemed to be the thing to do with them."

225

ARTIST: **BRAD HOLLAND**

ART DIRECTOR: Lew Fifield, Jim McCune

CLIENT: Maryland Institute College of Art

MEDIUM: Acrylic on Board

SIZE: 15x19

Born in 1952, Janet Woolley attended Brighton School of Art and the Royal College of Art in London. Her works have been exhibited at the Royal Academy, Portal Gallery, and Thumb Gallery London. Her many awards include the Berger Paint Award for Drawing, Sainsbury's Image for Today Illustration Poster Award, Benson & Hedges Gold Award, Society of Illustrators Gold and Silver Medals. Ms. Woolley teaches at St. Martin / Central School of Art in London.

226
ARTIST: **JANET WOOLLEY**
ART DIRECTOR: Tom Godici
AGENCY: Fred/Alan Inc.
CLIENT: MTV
MEDIUM: Acrylics, Printed Collage on Board
SIZE: 20x18

"For a number of years exploration into the potential applications of printmaking techniques, collage and adaptation of photographic elements into my illustrations have been an area of investigation.

The integration of unexpected elements juxtaposed with alien objects. The past and the future. Photo positives and negatives. The two dimensional and the three. The abstract and the concrete. New processes, at least for me, are areas of development and experimentation."

227

ARTIST: **FRED OTNES**

ART DIRECTOR: Fred Otnes

CLIENT: Artists Associates

MEDIUM: Mixed Media, Collage, Photo on Linen

SIZE: 17x11

228

ARTIST: **MARK McMAHON**

ART DIRECTOR: Bill Hereau

AGENCY: Bender Browning Dolby & Sanderson

CLIENT: Metra Transportation

MEDIUM: Watercolor, Acrylic, Pencil on Paper

SIZE: 23x30

229

ARTIST: **MARK McMAHON**

ART DIRECTOR: Bill Hereau

AGENCY: Bender Browning Dolby & Sanderson

CLIENT: Metra Transportation

MEDIUM: Watercolor, Acrylic, Pencil on Paper

SIZE: 26x40

230

ARTIST: **DEREK MUELLER**

ART DIRECTOR: Derek Mueller

MEDIUM: Oil on Board

SIZE: 23x36

231

ARTIST: **WAYNE McLOUGHLIN**

ART DIRECTOR: Wayne McLoughlin

MEDIUM: Acrylic on Masonite

SIZE: 23x45

228

229

230

231

232

ARTIST: **JAMES E. TENNISON**

ART DIRECTOR: Nancy Turner

CLIENT: The Fort Worth Ballet

MEDIUM: Oil on Canvas

SIZE: 42x32

233

ARTIST: **ANDRZEJ DUDZINSKI**

ART DIRECTOR: Susan Slover, Susan Huyser

CLIENT: Citicorp

MEDIUM: Pastel

SIZE: 19x39

234

ARTIST: **NEIL BRENNAN**

ART DIRECTOR: Allyson Hunter

AGENCY: Leo Burnett Co.

CLIENT: United Airlines

MEDIUM: Oil on Board

SIZE: 11x14

235

ARTIST: **BERNIE FUCHS**

ART DIRECTOR: Kent Alterman

CLIENT: Masterpiece Theater

MEDIUM: Oil on Canvas

SIZE: 35x23

232

233

234

235

236

ARTIST: **MARK A. FREDRICKSON**

ART DIRECTOR: Andrea Janetos-Hyett

AGENCY: Foote, Cone & Belding

CLIENT: Levi Strauss

MEDIUM: Acrylic

SIZE: 26x18

237

ARTIST: **MARK A. FREDRICKSON**

ART DIRECTOR: Andrea Janetos-Hyett

AGENCY: Foote, Cone & Belding

CLIENT: Levi Strauss

MEDIUM: Acrylic

SIZE: 26x18

238

ARTIST: **MARK A. FREDRICKSON**

ART DIRECTOR: Andrea Janetos-Hyett

AGENCY: Foote, Cone & Belding

CLIENT: Levi Strauss

MEDIUM: Acrylic

SIZE: 33x25

239

ARTIST: **HANK PARKER**

ART DIRECTOR: Hank Parker

MEDIUM: Graphite

SIZE: 18x24

237

238

239

240

ARTIST: **GERRY GERSTEN**

ART DIRECTOR: Len Slonevsky, Don Kahn

CLIENT: Schering Laboratories

MEDIUM: Paper Mâché Sculpture

SIZE: 14x13x13

241

ARTIST: **JOHN THOMPSON**

ART DIRECTOR: Stavros Cosmopulos, Rich Kerstein

AGENCY: Cosmopulos, Crowley & Daly

CLIENT: Allendale Insurance

MEDIUM: Acrylic on Board

SIZE: 13x23

242

ARTIST: **ERIC DINYER**

ART DIRECTOR: Brian Kroening

AGENCY: Campbell Mithun Esty

CLIENT: Empros

MEDIUM: Oil on Paper

SIZE: 14x11

243

ARTIST: **C.F. PAYNE**

ART DIRECTOR: Jim Baldwin

AGENCY: The Richards Group

CLIENT: T.G.I. Friday's

MEDIUM: Acrylic

SIZE: 17x15

240

241

242

243

244

ARTIST: **JONATHAN M. KNIGHT**

ART DIRECTOR: Charlie Robinson

CLIENT: George Washington Carver Center

MEDIUM: Pastel on Pastel Paper

SIZE: 10x10

245

ARTIST: **JON FLAMING**

ART DIRECTOR: Ron Sullivan

AGENCY: Sullivan Perkins

CLIENT: Westlake Center

MEDIUM: Airbrush, Color Overlays on Board

SIZE: 15x13

246

ARTIST: **LELAND KLANDERMAN**

ART DIRECTOR: Jack Thorwegen

AGENCY: Zipattoni Advertising

CLIENT: Chicken of the Sea

MEDIUM: Acrylic

SIZE: 30x40

247

ARTIST: **TONY WADE**

ART DIRECTOR: Joyce Mellow

CLIENT: Maritz Inc.

MEDIUM: Watercolor

SIZE: 5x6

244

245

246

247

248

ARTIST: **NORMAN WALKER**

ART DIRECTOR: Bill Erlacher

CLIENT: National Westminster Bank USA

MEDIUM: Oil

SIZE: 30x30

249

ARTIST: **ART GARCIA**

ART DIRECTOR: Ron Sullivan

CLIENT: Larry Wolf

MEDIUM: Photocopied Ink on Paper Towel

SIZE: 4x24

250

ARTIST: **JAMES McMULLAN**

ART DIRECTOR: Jim Russek

AGENCY: Russek Advertising

CLIENT: Lincoln Center

MEDIUM: Pastel on Paper

SIZE: 33x17

251

ARTIST: **SCOTT RAMSEY**

ART DIRECTOR: Scott Ramsey

CLIENT: San Diego Union Tribune

MEDIUM: Ink, Tape, Xerox

SIZE: 23x11

248

WOLF PACKS AGAIN   Alice, Larry and Richie, parrot Harry Bird, and cats Buster Mae Do

249

250

In 1542, Juan Cabrillo used the stars to discover San Diego.

251

n.D.J., Grizzabella, Renee Buckles, and Miss Kitty have moved (but not the horse, of course). You can now find them at 11224 Ridermark Row, Columbia, Maryland 21044.

252

ARTIST: **WILSON McLEAN**

ART DIRECTOR: Derek Smith

AGENCY: McCann Erickson

CLIENT: Esso

MEDIUM: Oil

SIZE: 25x20

253

ARTIST: **MALCOLM TARLOFSKY**

ART DIRECTOR: Nancy Donald

CLIENT: CBS Records

MEDIUM: Photo, Collage

SIZE: 18X6

254

ARTIST: **BRYAN L. PETERSON**

ART DIRECTOR: Bryan L. Peterson

CLIENT: Highland Village Fair Balloon Festival

MEDIUM: Silkscreen on Paper

SIZE: 22x16

255

ARTIST: **JEFF DODGE**

ART DIRECTOR: Janet Klein

CLIENT: Kansas City Star Co.

MEDIUM: Pastel on Paper

SIZE: 12x10

252

Hand of fate

253

254

255

256
ARTIST: **NEIL BRENNAN**
CLIENT: Susan Gomberg
MEDIUM: Oil on Board
SIZE: 12x17

257
ARTIST: **DAVE CUTLER**
ART DIRECTOR: Dave Cutler, Tina McGill, Craig Rathbum
CLIENT: Sharp Electronics Corporation
MEDIUM: Acrylic Collage on Paper
SIZE: 10x10

258
ARTIST: **BERNIE FUCHS**
ART DIRECTOR: John Steinbach
CLIENT: "Taylor Made"
MEDIUM: Oil on Canvas
SIZE: 23x37

259
ARTIST: **DANIEL MARK DUFFY**
ART DIRECTOR: Daniel Mark Duffy
MEDIUM: Graphite on Watercolor Paper
SIZE: 15x21

256

257

258

259

260

ARTIST: **KEVIN BURKE**

ART DIRECTOR: Greg Simmons

CLIENT: Zellerbach

MEDIUM: Oil, Acrylic on Coated Papers

SIZE: 19x13

261

ARTIST: **JANET WOOLLEY**

ART DIRECTOR: Richard Aguan

CLIENT: Villard Books

MEDIUM: Acrylic, Printed Collage on Board

SIZE: 17x23

262

ARTIST: **VIVIENNE FLESHER**

ART DIRECTOR: Richard Mantel

CLIENT: New York

MEDIUM: Pastel

SIZE: 15x11

263

ARTIST: **MARK RYDEN**

ART DIRECTOR: Mark Ryden

CLIENT: Chrysalis Records

MEDIUM: Acrylic on Board

SIZE: 10x9

260

261

262

263

264

ARTIST: **DANIEL CRAIG**

ART DIRECTOR: George Halvorson

AGENCY: Campbell Mithun Esty

CLIENT: United Way

MEDIUM: Acrylic on Board

SIZE: 34x30

265

ARTIST: **BART BEMUS**

ART DIRECTOR: Ron Hansen

AGENCY: Ron Hansen & Partners

CLIENT: The Seattle Aquarium

MEDIUM: Oil

SIZE: 17x28

266

ARTIST: **JOHN THOMPSON**

ART DIRECTOR: Jerry Demoney

CLIENT: Darwin Bahm

MEDIUM: Acrylic on Paper

SIZE: 23x16

267

ARTIST: **RAFAL OLBINSKI**

ART DIRECTOR: Jim Russek

CLIENT: Lincoln Center Theatre

MEDIUM: Acrylic on Canvas

SIZE: 18x13

264

265

266

267

268

ARTIST: **BART BEMUS**

ART DIRECTOR: Ron Hansen

AGENCY: Ron Hansen & Partners

CLIENT: Allied Printers

MEDIUM: Oil

SIZE: 24x19

269

ARTIST: **ALAN PHILLIPS**

ART DIRECTOR: Alan Phillips

MEDIUM: Oil on Canvas

SIZE: 27x30

270

ARTIST: **THOMAS AMOROSI**

ART DIRECTOR: Thomas Amorosi

MEDIUM: Colored Pencil on Board

SIZE: 15x12

271

ARTIST: **WARREN LINN**

ART DIRECTOR: Don Kahn

CLIENT: Schering Laboratories

MEDIUM: Acrylic, Collage on Board

SIZE: 16x14

268

269

270

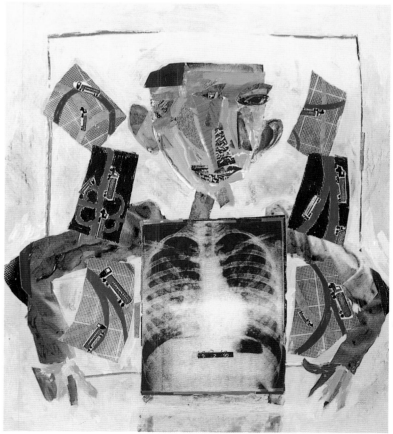

271

272

ARTIST: **GARY HEAD**

ART DIRECTOR: Nancy Ornce

CLIENT: Hallmark Cards, Inc.

MEDIUM: Pastel on Paper

SIZE: 15x12

273

ARTIST: **JAMES TUGHAN**

ART DIRECTOR: Glen Fretz, James Tughan

CLIENT: Ontario Real Estate Association

MEDIUM: Pastel on Watercolor Paper

SIZE: 13x28

274

ARTIST: **GARY KELLEY**

ART DIRECTOR: Rita Marshall

CLIENT: Creative Education

MEDIUM: Pastel on Paper

SIZE: 21x14

275

ARTIST: **GARY KELLEY**

ART DIRECTOR: Alf Zusi

AGENCY: S.J. Weinstein Assoc.

CLIENT: Searle

MEDIUM: Pastel on Paper

SIZE: 21x16

272

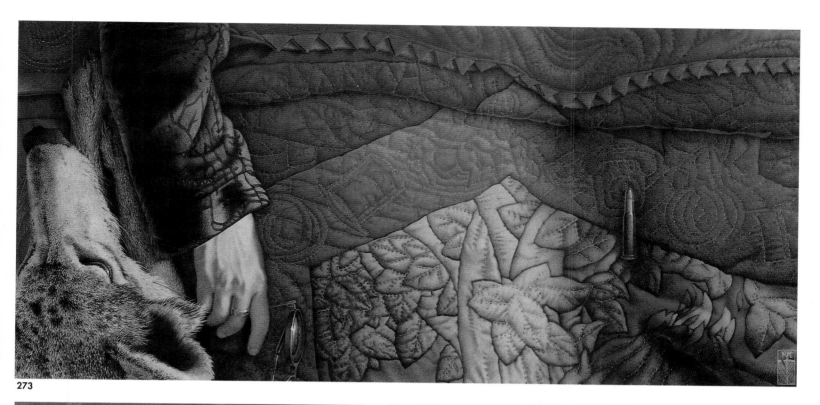

273

274

275

276
ARTIST: **MIKE HODGES**
ART DIRECTOR: Gary Kasmerick
AGENCY: Hutcheson-Shutze
CLIENT: Lettuce Souprise You
MEDIUM: Acrylic, Alkyds on Paper
SIZE: 15x11

277
ARTIST: **JACK UNRUH**
ART DIRECTOR: Nora Magee
AGENCY: McCaffrey & McCall
CLIENT: Westvaco
MEDIUM: Ink, Watercolor, Stamps on Board
SIZE: 15x22

278
ARTIST: **JACK UNRUH**
ART DIRECTOR: Chris Hill
CLIENT: Wildcat Ranch
MEDIUM: Ink, Watercolor on Board
SIZE: 16x11

279
ARTIST: **JACK UNRUH**
ART DIRECTOR: Chris Hill
CLIENT: Wildcat Ranch
MEDIUM: Ink, Watercolor on Board
SIZE: 16x11

276

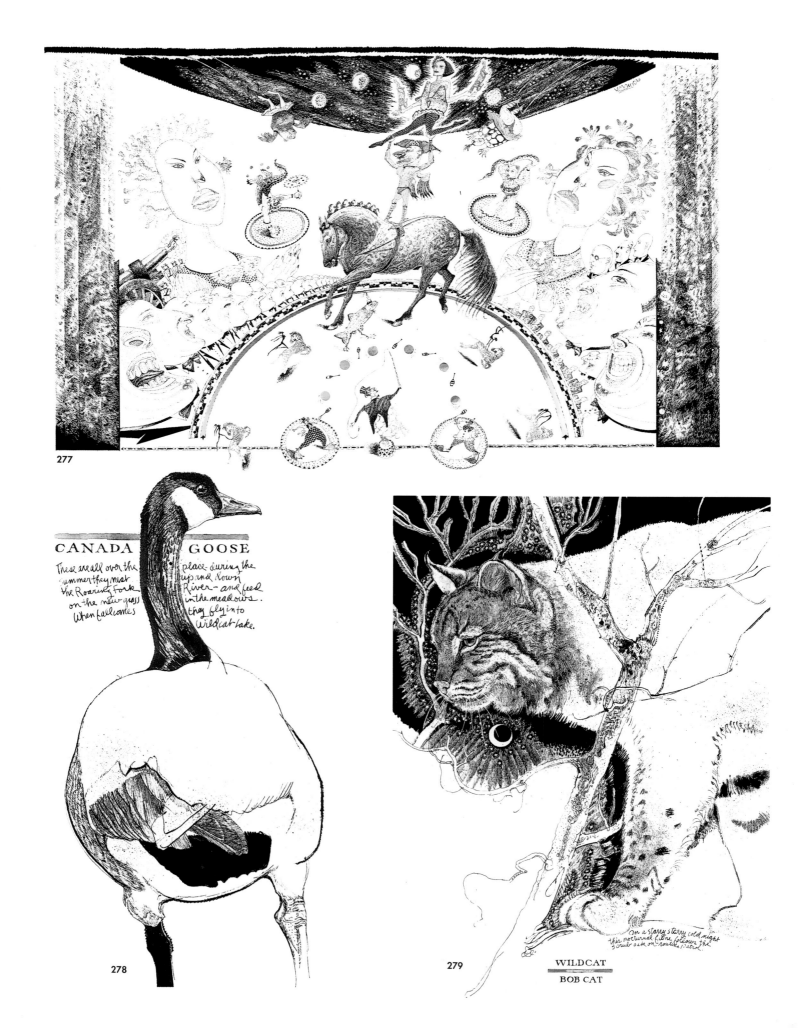

277

CANADA GOOSE

These are all over the place during the summer they nest up and down the Roaring Fork River - and feed on the new grass in the meadows. When fall comes they fly into Wildcat Lake.

278

279

In a starry starry cold night this nocturnal feline glows scrub oak on route 1 patrol

WILDCAT

BOB CAT

280

ARTIST: **BART FORBES**

ART DIRECTOR: Bart Marantz

CLIENT: Arts Jazz

MEDIUM: Oil on Canvas

SIZE: 26x19

281

ARTIST: **DOUGLAS FRASER**

ART DIRECTOR: Matt Canzano

AGENCY: J. Walter Thompson

CLIENT: Lowenbrau

MEDIUM: Alkyds on Paper

SIZE: 14x24

282

ARTIST: **DOUGLAS FRASER**

ART DIRECTOR: Matt Canzano

AGENCY: J. Walter Thompson

CLIENT: Lowenbrau

MEDIUM: Alkyds on Paper

SIZE: 18x16

283

ARTIST: **DOUGLAS FRASER**

ART DIRECTOR: Matt Canzano

AGENCY: J. Walter Thompson

CLIENT: Lowenbrau

MEDIUM: Alkyds on Paper

SIZE: 22x16

280

281

282

283

284

ARTIST: **JOHN COLLIER**

ART DIRECTOR: Neal Pozner

AGENCY: Russek Advertising

CLIENT: The Joyce Theater

MEDIUM: Oil

SIZE: 30x36

285

ARTIST: **JOHN COLLIER**

ART DIRECTOR: Neal Pozner

AGENCY: Russek Advertising

CLIENT: The Joyce Theater

MEDIUM: Oil

SIZE: 7x11

286

ARTIST: **BRALDT BRALDS**

ART DIRECTOR: Terri Freeberg

CLIENT: Minneapolis Public Library

MEDIUM: Oil on Masonite

SIZE: 10x17

287

ARTIST: **BRALDT BRALDS**

ART DIRECTOR: Alice McKown

CLIENT: Western Microtechnology/Data General

MEDIUM: Oil on Masonite

SIZE: 15x29

284

285

286

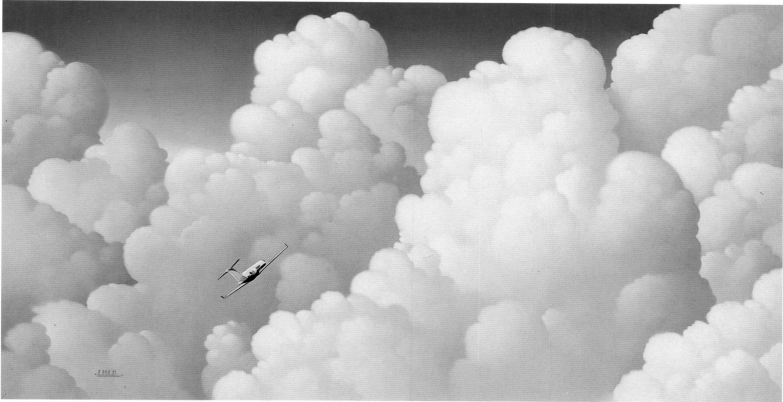

287

288

ARTIST: **RAFAL OLBINSKI**

ART DIRECTOR: Albert Leutwyler

CLIENT: Equitable Capital Management Corporation

MEDIUM: Acrylic

SIZE: 15x13

289

ARTIST: **BOB PETERS**

ART DIRECTOR: Scott Lambert

CLIENT: Intel

MEDIUM: Acrylic on Board

SIZE: 11x21

290

ARTIST: **MARK ENGLISH**

ART DIRECTOR: Mark English

MEDIUM: Oil

SIZE: 43x36

291

ARTIST: **DAVID LESH**

ART DIRECTOR: Janis Brown

CLIENT: Birtcher

MEDIUM: Mixed Media

SIZE: 12x9

288

289

290

291

292

ARTIST: **JOHN HARRIS**

ART DIRECTOR: Tom Egner

CLIENT: Avon Books

MEDIUM: Ink, Acrylic on Board

SIZE: 19x12

293

ARTIST: **ETIENNE DELESSERT**

ART DIRECTOR: Etienne Delessert

CLIENT: Henri Des

MEDIUM: Watercolor

SIZE: 12x12

294

ARTIST: **ETIENNE DELESSERT**

ART DIRECTOR: George Pollack

AGENCY: Evans, Bartholomew Denver

CLIENT: Coors

MEDIUM: Watercolor

SIZE: 9x8

295

ARTIST: **ETIENNE DELESSERT**

ART DIRECTOR: Etienne Delessert

CLIENT: Henri Des

MEDIUM: Watercolor

SIZE: 12x12

293

294

295

296

ARTIST: **JOHN MARTIN**

ART DIRECTOR: Mark Krumel

AGENCY: Rickabaugh Graphics

CLIENT: Roxanne Labs

MEDIUM: Acrylic

SIZE: 13x10

297

ARTIST: **COLIN POOLE**

ART DIRECTOR: Colin Poole

MEDIUM: Acrylic, Dyes, Watercolor on Board

SIZE: 10x19

298

ARTIST: **RICHARD WEHRMAN**

ART DIRECTOR: Jeff Marinelli

CLIENT: Illustrator's Forum

MEDIUM: Pencil, Gouache, Ink on Paper

SIZE: 10x8

299

ARTIST: **RICHARD WEHRMAN**

ART DIRECTOR: Richard Wehrman

CLIENT: Corn Hill Neighbors Inc.

MEDIUM: Acrylic on Board

SIZE: 23x15

296

297

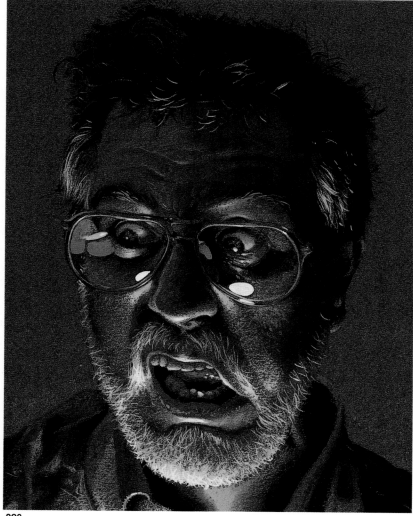

298

299

300
ARTIST: **BRAD HOLLAND**
ART DIRECTOR: Brad Holland, Jim McCune
CLIENT: Art Directors Association of Iowa
MEDIUM: Acrylic on Masonite
SIZE: 14x11

301
ARTIST: **CURT DOTY**
ART DIRECTOR: Jim Miller
CLIENT: AT&T
MEDIUM: Oil on Watercolor Paper
SIZE: 23x16

302
ARTIST: **CURTIS PARKER**
ART DIRECTOR: Art Lofgreen
MEDIUM: Watercolor, Bleach, Airbrush
SIZE: 28x19

303
ARTIST: **ED PARKER**
ART DIRECTOR: Kathy Aromando
AGENCY: Darcy Masius Benton & Bowles
CLIENT: Maxwell House
MEDIUM: Acrylic, Varnish on Masonite
SIZE: 11x25

300

301

302

REDISCOVER · SLOW · ROASTED · TASTE

303

304

ARTIST: **RICHARD MANTEL**

ART DIRECTOR: Richard Mantel

CLIENT: The Hampton Classic

MEDIUM: Acrylic on Masonite

SIZE: 20x18

305

ARTIST: **MARK CHICKINELLI**

ART DIRECTOR: Janeen Macrino

CLIENT: Omaha Ballet

MEDIUM: Acrylic, Serigraph on Board

SIZE: 23x21

306

ARTIST: **MURRAY TINKELMAN**

ART DIRECTOR: Murray Tinkelman

MEDIUM: Pen and Ink Etching

SIZE: 25x19

307

ARTIST: **MICHAEL HALBERT**

ART DIRECTOR: Debra Harstead

AGENCY: BKM & M

CLIENT: Henry Ford Museum & Greenfield Village

MEDIUM: Scratchboard and Pen

SIZE: 10x17

304

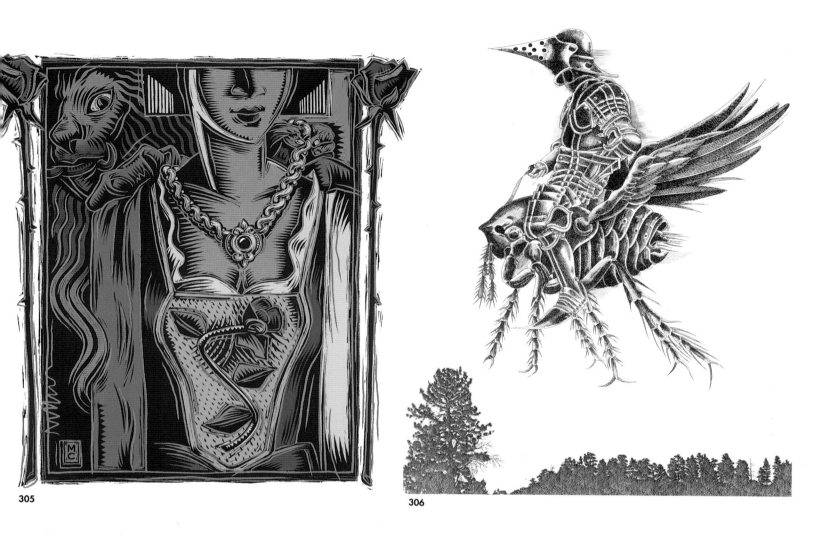

305

306

307

308

ARTIST: **WILSON McLEAN**

ART DIRECTOR: Albert Leutwyler

CLIENT: Equitable Capital Management Corporation

MEDIUM: Oil on Canvas

SIZE: 22x18

309

ARTIST: **CORBERT GAUTHIER**

ART DIRECTOR: Becky Bjornson

CLIENT: Lifetouch National School Studios, Inc.

MEDIUM: Oil

SIZE: 16x28

310

ARTIST: **DAVE CUTLER**

ART DIRECTOR: John Goecke, Randy Miller

CLIENT: Share Our Strength

MEDIUM: Oil, Collage on Watercolor Paper

SIZE: 25x17

311

ARTIST: **MARSHALL ARISMAN**

ART DIRECTOR: Robert Raines

CLIENT: Book-of-the-Month Club

MEDIUM: Acrylic

SIZE: 28x23

308

309

310

311

312
ARTIST: **CHRIS CONSANI**
ART DIRECTOR: Avi Semo, Bob Pitt
AGENCY: BBDO Atlanta
CLIENT: Delta Airlines/Air Cargo
MEDIUM: Acrylic
SIZE: 19x19

313
ARTIST: **JOYCE KITCHELL**
ART DIRECTOR: Pat Chin
AGENCY: Cline Davis & Mann, Inc.
CLIENT: Pfizer Pharmaceuticals
MEDIUM: Watercolor on Paper
SIZE: 19x18

314
ARTIST: **CURTIS PARKER**
ART DIRECTOR: Jordan Barrett
AGENCY: Jordan Barrett Assoc.
CLIENT: Capital Bancorp
MEDIUM: Watercolor, Bleach, Airbrush
SIZE: 8x20

315
ARTIST: **ED PARKER**
ART DIRECTOR: Linda Richee
CLIENT: Polaroid
MEDIUM: Acrylic, Varnish on Masonite
SIZE: 9x7

312

313

314

315

316

ARTIST: **CHRIS HOPKINS**

ART DIRECTOR: Chris Hopkins

CLIENT: Travamerica

MEDIUM: Oil on Board

SIZE: 34x24

317

ARTIST: **MARVIN MATTELSON**

ART DIRECTOR: Dave Diatkowski

AGENCY: Backer Speilvogel Bates

CLIENT: Benson & Hedges

MEDIUM: Acrylic

SIZE: 10x16

318

ARTIST: **DAVID LUI**

ART DIRECTOR: Susan Newman

CLIENT: Step-by-Step Graphics

MEDIUM: Collage

SIZE: 22x16

319

ARTIST: **BRAD HOLLAND**

ART DIRECTOR: Ken Neiheisel

CLIENT: Art Directors Club of Cincinnati

MEDIUM: Acrylic on Masonite

SIZE: 16x20

316

317

318

319

320

ARTIST: **EDWARD SOREL**

ART DIRECTOR: Neal Pozner

AGENCY: Russek Advertising

CLIENT: Lincoln Center Theatre

MEDIUM: Pen, Ink, Watercolor on Paper

SIZE: 24x16

321

ARTIST: **DAVID LUI**

ART DIRECTOR: David Lui

CLIENT: Step-by-Step Graphics

MEDIUM: Collage

SIZE: 16x27

322

ARTIST: **RICHARD SPARKS**

ART DIRECTOR: Ria Lewerke

AGENCY: MBG/RCA

CLIENT: RCA

MEDIUM: Oil on Linen

SIZE: 16x16

323

ARTIST: **PAUL DAVIS**

ART DIRECTOR: Fran Michelman

CLIENT: Mobil Masterpiece Theater

MEDIUM: Acrylic on Wood

SIZE: 19x14

321

322

323

324

ARTIST: **BILL NELSON**

ART DIRECTOR: Bill Nelson, Louise Fili

CLIENT: Richard Solomon

MEDIUM: Colored Pencil on Board

SIZE: 13x10

325

ARTIST: **ROBERT CRAIG**

ART DIRECTOR: Robert Craig

CLIENT: Ciba-Geigy

MEDIUM: Dyes, Acrylic on Blue Print Paper

SIZE: 17x21

326

ARTIST: **SEYMOUR CHWAST**

ART DIRECTOR: Ivan Chermayeff, Jane Clark Chermayeff

CLIENT: International Design Conference of Aspen

MEDIUM: Pencil, Acrylic on Brown Paper

SIZE: 23x16

327

ARTIST: **TOM CURRY**

ART DIRECTOR: Kate Johnson

CLIENT: Netware Technical Journal

MEDIUM: Acrylic Drybrush on Mylar

SIZE: 11x11

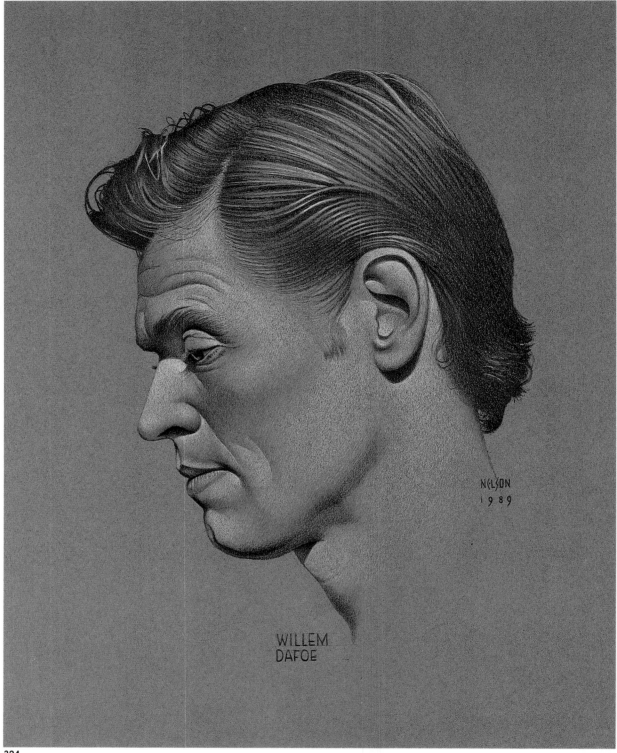

324

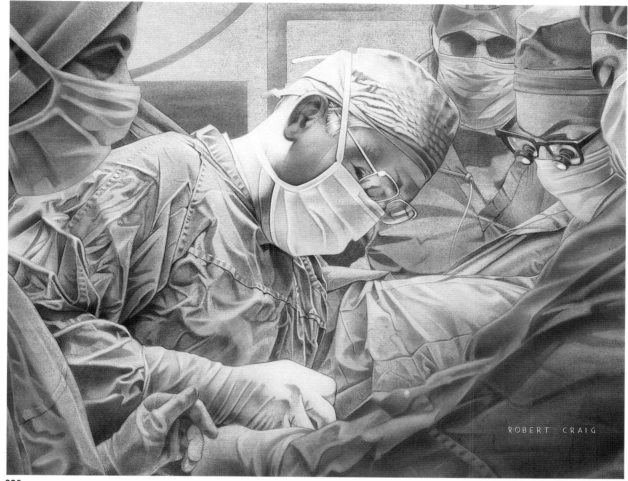

325

326

327

328

ARTIST: **LISA FRENCH**

ART DIRECTOR: Chris Chaffin

AGENCY: Hal Riney & Partners

CLIENT: See's Candies

MEDIUM: Acrylic, Blue Print on Board

SIZE: 10x13

329

ARTIST: **ALAN E. COBER**

ART DIRECTOR: Albert Gregory

CLIENT: G.E. Capital

MEDIUM: Ink, Watercolor, Prisma Color

SIZE: 12x18

330

ARTIST: **TIM O'BRIEN**

ART DIRECTOR: Tim O'Brien

MEDIUM: Oil on Board

SIZE: 19x17

331

ARTIST: **CURT DOTY**

ART DIRECTOR: Margaret Wollenhaupt

CLIENT: Champion Paper

MEDIUM: Oil on Watercolor Paper

SIZE: 14x12

328

329

330

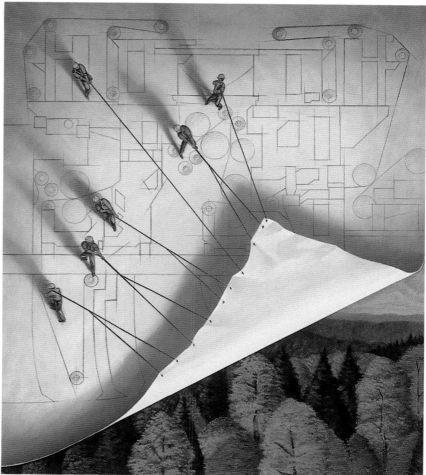

331

332

ARTIST: **MARVIN MATTELSON**

ART DIRECTOR: Tom Godici

AGENCY: Fred/Alan Inc.

CLIENT: MTV

MEDIUM: Acrylic

SIZE: 11x10

333

ARTIST: **BERNIE FUCHS**

ART DIRECTOR: John Steinbach

CLIENT: "Taylor Made"

MEDIUM: Oil on Canvas

SIZE: 23x38

334

ARTIST: **MARK RYDEN**

ART DIRECTOR: Kevin Hosmann

CLIENT: Metal Blade Records

MEDIUM: Acrylic on Paper

SIZE: 15x15

335

ARTIST: **DAVID LUI**

ART DIRECTOR: David Lui

CLIENT: How Magazine

MEDIUM: Collage

SIZE: 19x19

332

333

334

335

336
ARTIST: **JOEL PETER JOHNSON**
ART DIRECTOR: Helen Garrett
CLIENT: Amnesty International
MEDIUM: Oil, Graphite
SIZE: 16x13

337
ARTIST: **TIM HILDEBRANDT**
ART DIRECTOR: Tim Hildebrandt
MEDIUM: Acrylic on Masonite
SIZE: 32x60

338
ARTIST: **DOUGLAS BEVANS**
ART DIRECTOR: Stephen Meltzer
CLIENT: Motown Records, L.P.
MEDIUM: Papercut, Charcoal Paper, Board
SIZE: 14x11

339
ARTIST: **TERRY WIDENER**
ART DIRECTOR: Richard Mantel
CLIENT: New York
MEDIUM: Acrylic on Canvas
SIZE: 17x12

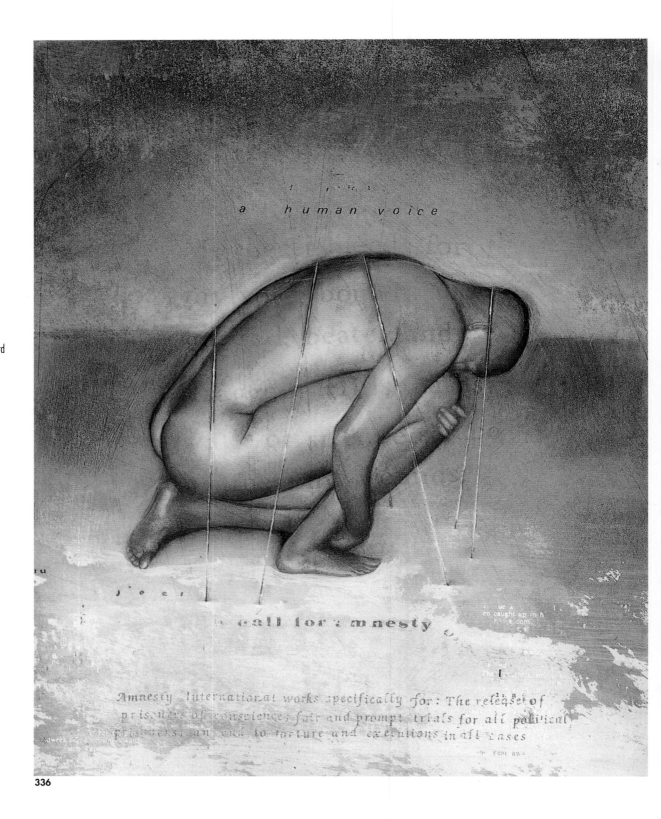

336

337

338

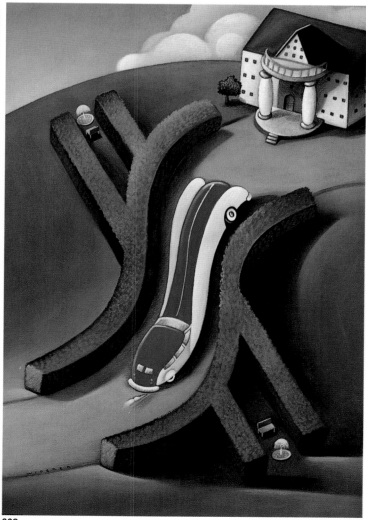

339

340

ARTIST: **H.B. LEWIS**

ART DIRECTOR: Mary Arzt

AGENCY: Wietzman & Livingston

CLIENT: Washington Hilton

MEDIUM: Gouache, Colored Pencil on Paper

SIZE: 13x11

341

ARTIST: **RICHARD SPARKS**

ART DIRECTOR: Maria Rubino

AGENCY: MBI Inc.

CLIENT: MBI Inc.

MEDIUM: Oil on Paper

SIZE: 12x17

342

ARTIST: **ALAN E. COBER**

ART DIRECTOR: Bill Shinn

CLIENT: Case Western Reserve

MEDIUM: Ink, Watercolor, Prisma Color

SIZE: 11x8

343

ARTIST: **RICHARD SPARKS**

ART DIRECTOR: Ria Lewerke

AGENCY: MBG/RCA

CLIENT: RCA

MEDIUM: Watercolor on Linen

SIZE: 27x24

340

341

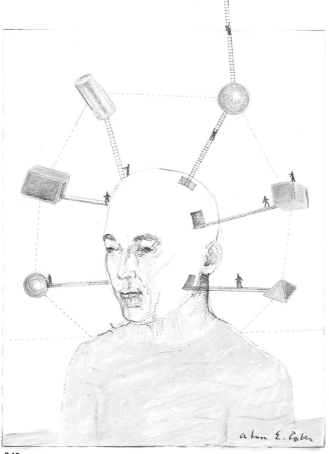

342

343

INSTITUTIONAL JURY

Bernie D'Andrea
CHAIRMAN; ILLUSTRATOR, PAINTER

Donald Bender
CREATIVE DIRECTOR, OUTLET BOOKS, RANDOM HOUSE

Grace Clarke
VICE PRESIDENT/EDITOR IN CHIEF, CHILDREN'S BOOK DIVISION
SIMON & SCHUSTER

B. W. Honeycutt
ART DIRECTOR, *SPY MAGAZINE*

Catherine Huerta
ILLUSTRATOR

Roger Kastel
ILLUSTRATOR

Lane Smith
ILLUSTRATOR

Richard Sparks
ILLUSTRATOR

Richard Wehrman
ILLUSTRATOR, THE BOB WRIGHT CREATIVE GROUP

William Hillenbrand
GOLD MEDAL

Brad Holland
GOLD MEDAL

Kinuko Y. Craft
SILVER MEDAL

Gary Kelley
SILVER MEDAL

Bryan Leister
SILVER MEDAL

INSTITUTIONAL

WILLIAM HILLENBRAND

A native of Cincinnati, Ohio, Hillenbrand graduated from the Art Academy of Cincinnati. Prior to becoming a freelance illustrator, he worked as an art director for an advertising agency. He is now illustrating children's books and working on a series of paintings depicting rowing subjects for Champion International. Hillenbrand has received awards from *Communication Arts*, the Society of Publication Designers, *Advertising Age*, *Print*, and the Society of Illustrators.

344

ARTIST: **WILLIAM HILLENBRAND**

ART DIRECTOR: Bart Crosby

CLIENT: Champion International Corporation

MEDIUM: Oil on Linen

SIZE: 16x23

"I've learned that people going from New York to Atlantic City to gamble get into a reckless frame of mind by driving there. The first leg of the trip I drove with a carload of Jamaicans who were plenty reckless to begin with. It was bumper-cars all the way. I wandered around the casinos until dawn, sketching—mostly at Bally's where the carpets were red and the craps dealer looked like a genie who had just escaped from his lamp.

"In Vegas they don't have clocks; you can gamble all night. Women perform nude, men perform as women and prostitutes hand out throwaways at street corners. At the Frontier Casino security men saw me drawing and followed me with walkie talkies. They stopped me, questioned me, tried to confiscate my sketchbook and finally kicked me out. I think it's reassuring that there are still some things you can't get away with in Vegas."

345

ARTIST: **BRAD HOLLAND**
ART DIRECTOR: Scott Taylor, Paul Campbell
CLIENT: Norgraphics (Canada) Limited
MEDIUM: Acrylic on Masonite
SIZE: 18x25

346
ARTIST: **BRYAN LEISTER**
ART DIRECTOR: Chris Noel
CLIENT: The Smithsonian Institution Traveling
Exhibition Service (SITES)
MEDIUM: Oil
SIZE: 17x25

"I have a friend who plays polo. It's a colorful sport happening outside the mainstream. That intrigues me. My father died of cancer. He loved horses. This poster art was created free of charge for the Cancer Society. Don't ever smoke."

347
ARTIST: **GARY KELLEY**
ART DIRECTOR: Bill Oxford
CLIENT: American Cancer Society
MEDIUM: Pastel on Paper
SIZE: 24x15

348
ARTIST: **KINUKO Y. CRAFT**
ART DIRECTOR: Clay Freeman
CLIENT: The Washington Opera
MEDIUM: Oil
SIZE: 16x12

349

ARTIST: **MICHAEL PARASKEVAS**

MEDIUM: Acrylic on Paper

SIZE: 18x24

350

ARTIST: **KENT WILLIAMS**

ART DIRECTOR: Kent Williams

MEDIUM: Mixed Media on Paper

SIZE: 22x22

351

ARTIST: **MITCHELL HEINZE**

ART DIRECTOR: Mitchell Heinze

MEDIUM: Acrylic

SIZE: 24x32

352

ARTIST: **JEFFREY OH**

ART DIRECTOR: David Crowder

CLIENT: Baltimore Zoo

MEDIUM: Dyes, Watercolor, Pencil on Board

SIZE: 24x29

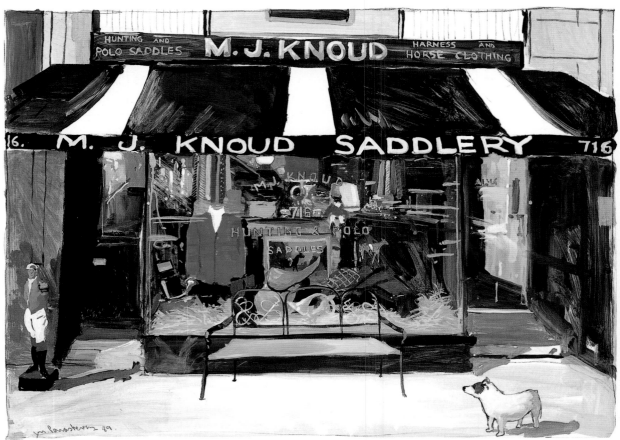

349

350

351

352

353

ARTIST: **PAUL DAVIS**

ART DIRECTOR: Silas Rhodes

CLIENT: Visual Arts Museum

MEDIUM: Wood, Metal, Rubber, Paint on Wood

SIZE: 24x17

354

ARTIST: **JOANNE HOFFMAN**

ART DIRECTOR: Joanne Hoffman

CLIENT: Balch Institute of Ethnic Studies

MEDIUM: Mixed Media

SIZE: 3'x6'

355

ARTIST: **JOHN H. HOWARD**

ART DIRECTOR: Marjorie Millyard

CLIENT: Arkwright Mutual Insurance Company

MEDIUM: Acrylic on Canvas

SIZE: 20x16

356

ARTIST: **JOHN H. HOWARD**

ART DIRECTOR: Morris Taub

MEDIUM: Acrylic on Canvas

SIZE: 16x12

353

354

355

356

357

ARTIST: **JOHN P. MAGGARD III**

ART DIRECTOR: Karen Abney, Bruce Huninghake

CLIENT: Abney/Huninghake Design

MEDIUM: Pencil, Acrylic, Oil on Board

SIZE: 19x15

358

ARTIST: **JOHN P. MAGGARD III**

ART DIRECTOR: John P. Maggard III, Cliff Schwandner

CLIENT: Cincinnati Heart Assoc./American Heart Assoc.

MEDIUM: Acrylic, Oil, Ink on Board

SIZE: 34x13

359

ARTIST: **ALBERT LORENZ**

ART DIRECTOR: Albert Lorenz

MEDIUM: Pen, Ink, Watercolor Pencil on Board

SIZE: 39x30

360

ARTIST: **ALBERT LORENZ**

ART DIRECTOR: Albert Lorenz

CLIENT: Pratt Institute

MEDIUM: Pen, Ink, Colored Pencil on Board

SIZE: 36x24

357

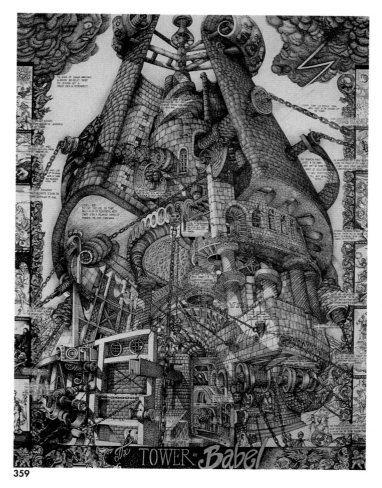

359

361

ARTIST: **WARREN GEBERT**

ART DIRECTOR: Kathy Grubb

AGENCY: Gray Baumgarten Layport, Inc.

CLIENT: Parker/Hunter Inc.

MEDIUM: Pastel, Tempera

SIZE: 16x12

362

ARTIST: **CYNTHIA TORP**

ART DIRECTOR: Ken Herndon

CLIENT: Humana Festival of New American Plays

MEDIUM: Acrylic and Prisma Color

SIZE: 52X72

363

ARTIST: **BRIAN FOX**

ART DIRECTOR: Brian Fox

MEDIUM: Charcoal on Paper

SIZE: 25x21

364

ARTIST: **M. JOHN ENGLISH**

ART DIRECTOR: Craig Franke

AGENCY: Frink Semmers & Associate

CLIENT: 3M

MEDIUM: Oil, Colored Pencil

SIZE: 24x18

361

362

363

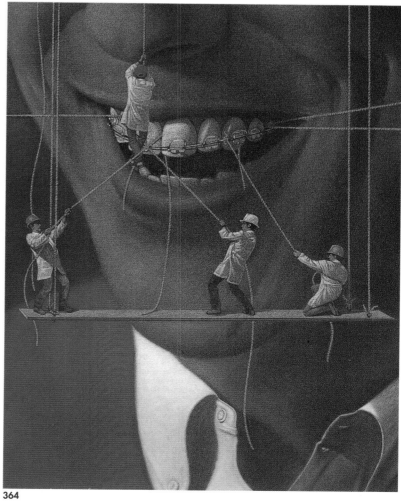

364

365
ARTIST: **DEBORAH HEALY**
ART DIRECTOR: Toni Markiet
CLIENT: HarperCollins Publishers
MEDIUM: Oil on Board
SIZE: 12x9

366
ARTIST: **BRAD HOLLAND**
ART DIRECTOR: Jennifer Phillips
CLIENT: New School for Social Research
MEDIUM: Acrylic on Masonite
SIZE: 13x20

367
ARTIST: **ROY PENDLETON**
ART DIRECTOR: Bill Freeland
CLIENT: LaGuardia Community College
MEDIUM: Acrylic on Canvas
SIZE: 24x15

368
ARTIST: **KEN WESTPHAL**
ART DIRECTOR: Ken Westphal
MEDIUM: Acrylic, Airbrush on Board
SIZE: 12x9

365

366

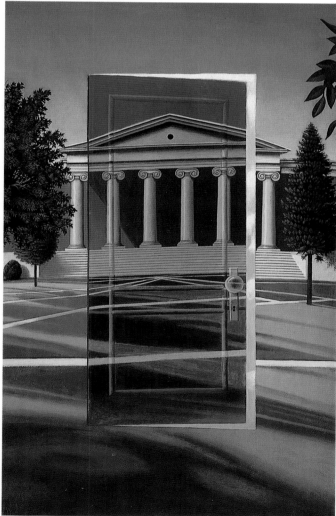

367

368

369

ARTIST: **M. JOHN ENGLISH**

ART DIRECTOR: M. John English

CLIENT: Avon

MEDIUM: Oil

SIZE: 30x38

370

ARTIST: **JÖZEF SUMICHRAST**

ART DIRECTOR: Robert Valentine

CLIENT: Bloomingdale's

MEDIUM: Transparent Dye

SIZE: 17x15

371

ARTIST: **BILL NELSON**

ART DIRECTOR: S. Samuelson

AGENCY: Lintas MCM

CLIENT: IBM

MEDIUM: Colored Pencil, Airbrush on Board

SIZE: 14x22

372

ARTIST: **ALEXA GRACE**

ART DIRECTOR: Mitsutoshi Hosaka

CLIENT: Matsuzaki Shoji

MEDIUM: Porcelain Paint

SIZE: 11x13

369

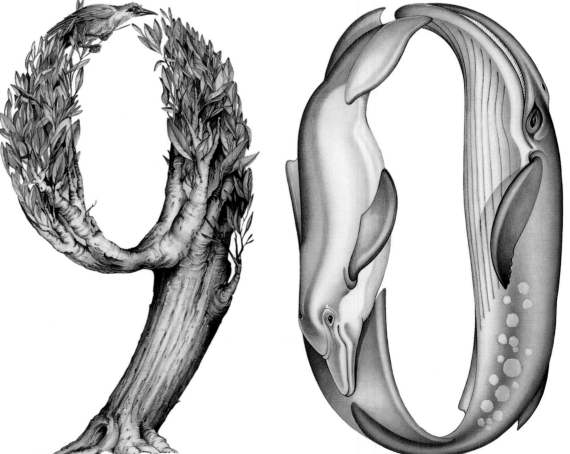

370

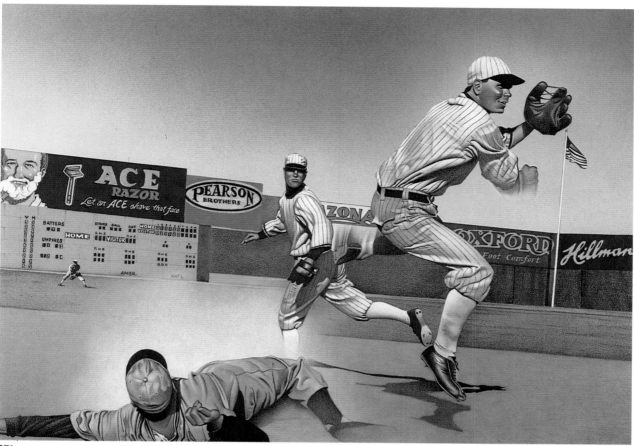

371

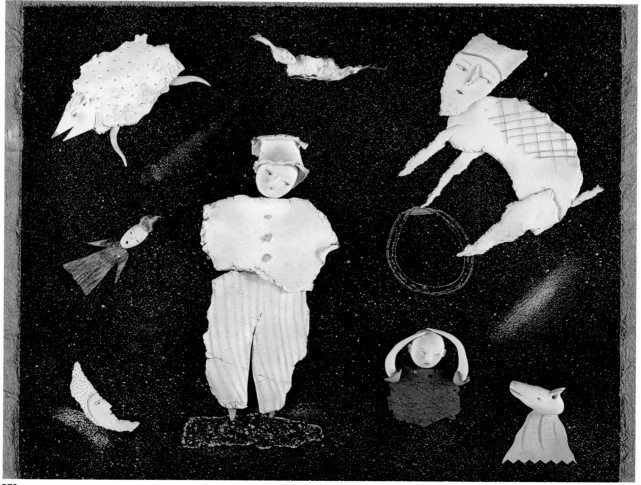

372

373

ARTIST: **JON J MUTH**

ART DIRECTOR: Jon J Muth

CLIENT: Allen Spiegel Fine Arts/August Co.

MEDIUM: Charcoal, Pastel, Silverpoint on Board

SIZE: 19x13

374

ARTIST: **WENDELL MINOR**

ART DIRECTOR: Pete Aguamono

CLIENT: American Movie Classics

MEDIUM: Acrylic on Masonite

SIZE: 18x27

375

ARTIST: **CHERYL COOPER**

ART DIRECTOR: Pete Rundquist, Julie Horner

CLIENT: IBM

MEDIUM: Oil

SIZE: 27x22

376

ARTIST: **JOSEF RUBINSTEIN**

ART DIRECTOR: Josef Rubinstein

MEDIUM: Oil on Canvas

SIZE: 23x17

373

374

375

376

377

ARTIST: **CATHERINE HUERTA**

ART DIRECTOR: Catherine Huerta

MEDIUM: Pencil, Acrylic, Oil on Board

SIZE: 23x23

378

ARTIST: **MARK McMAHON**

ART DIRECTOR: John Hammerschlag

CLIENT: General Parking Corp.

MEDIUM: Pencil Drawing Transfered to Tile

SIZE: 8'x 125'

379

ARTIST: **DOUGLAS FRASER**

ART DIRECTOR: Joseph Napolitano

CLIENT: The Creative Black Book

MEDIUM: Alkyds on Paper

SIZE: 12x7

380

ARTIST: **DOUGLAS FRASER**

ART DIRECTOR: Joseph Napolitano

CLIENT: The Creative Black Book

MEDIUM: Alkyds on Paper

SIZE: 11x7

377

378

379

380

381
ARTIST: **MARY GRANDPRE**
ART DIRECTOR: Mary Grandpre
CLIENT: Chargo Printing
MEDIUM: Pastel on Paper
SIZE: 13x13

382
ARTIST: **ANTHONY RUSSO**
ART DIRECTOR: Mitsutoshi Hosaka
CLIENT: Matsuzaki Shoji
SIZE: 13x13

383
ARTIST: **JIM HARRIS**
ART DIRECTOR: Carol Stickley
CLIENT: AMI San Dimas Community Hospital
MEDIUM: Acrylic
SIZE: 25x33

384
ARTIST: **DEAN KENNEDY**
ART DIRECTOR: Tony Luetkehans
CLIENT: Hellman Associates
MEDIUM: Oil on Board
SIZE: 17x15

385
ARTIST: **KIM BEHM**
ART DIRECTOR: Tony Luetkehans
CLIENT: Hellman Associates
MEDIUM: Oil
SIZE: 27x20

381

382

383

384

385

386

ARTIST: **TIM O'BRIEN**

ART DIRECTOR: Tim O'Brien

MEDIUM: Oil on Board

SIZE: 21x18

387

ARTIST: **HODGES SOILEAU**

ART DIRECTOR: Hodges Soileau

MEDIUM: Oil on Canvas

SIZE: 32x38

388

ARTIST: **ROBERT G. STEELE**

MEDIUM: Watercolor on Watercolor Paper

SIZE: 16x11

389

ARTIST: **ALAN FLINN**

ART DIRECTOR: Alan Flinn

CLIENT: Theatreworks/University of Colorado

MEDIUM: Gouache on Board

SIZE: 16x13

386

387

388

389

390

ARTIST: **LINDA DEVITO**

ART DIRECTOR: Paul Bilsky, Linda Devito

CLIENT: The Stephen Lawrence Co.

MEDIUM: Oil on Canvas

SIZE: 9x14

391

ARTIST: **JAMES DIETZ**

ART DIRECTOR: Bill Campbell, Bruce Roberts

CLIENT: Allison Turbine/Transmissions

MEDIUM: Oil on Canvas

SIZE: 29x40

392

ARTIST: **DAVID K. STONE**

ART DIRECTOR: James Helzer

CLIENT: Unicover Corp.

MEDIUM: Oil on Masonite

SIZE: 17x21

393

ARTIST: **ROY THOMPSON**

ART DIRECTOR: Roy Thompson

MEDIUM: Acrylic

SIZE: 14x18

390

391

392

393

394
ARTIST: **ANNIE LUNSFORD**
ART DIRECTOR: Bono Mitchell
CLIENT: Bruce Printing Inc.
MEDIUM: Alkyds, Oil on Board
SIZE: 24x13

395
ARTIST: **GRIESBACH/MARTUCCI**
ART DIRECTOR: Thomasina Webb
CLIENT: Jacqueline Dedell Inc.
MEDIUM: Oil on Masonite
SIZE: 12x20

396
ARTIST: **RED GROOMS**
ART DIRECTOR: Cliff Sloan, Debbie Millman, Noreen Pero
CLIENT: National Dance Institute

397
ARTIST: **DREW BISHOP**
MEDIUM: Oil on Masonite
SIZE: 15x11

394

395

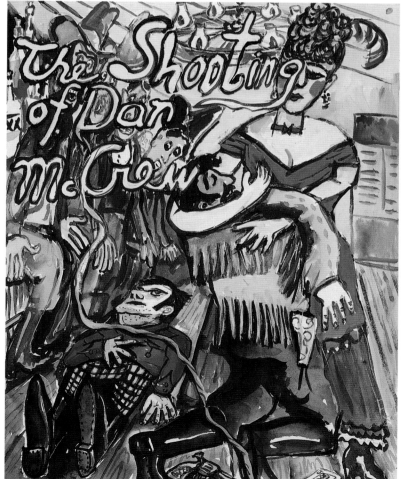

396

397

398
ARTIST: **KINUKO Y. CRAFT**
ART DIRECTOR: Alice Degenhardt
CLIENT: North Western Mutual Life Insurance
MEDIUM: Oil, Watercolor on Board
SIZE: 21x18

399
ARTIST: **JOHN SAYLES**
ART DIRECTOR: John Sayles
CLIENT: Midland United Dairy Industry Association
MEDIUM: Ink, Offset Lithography on Vellum
SIZE: 38x17

400
ARTIST: **JOHN THOMPSON**
ART DIRECTOR: John Thompson
CLIENT: U.S. Air Force
MEDIUM: Acrylic on Chip Board
SIZE: 15x12

401
ARTIST: **JOHN THOMPSON**
CLIENT: The United Nations
MEDIUM: Acrylic on Rag Board
SIZE: 34x27

398

399

400

401

402

ARTIST: **RON BELL**

ART DIRECTOR: Lisa Ballard

CLIENT: NCR Computers

MEDIUM: Gouache, Pastel, Pencil on Paper

SIZE: 9x8

403

ARTIST: **ARDEN VON HAEGER**

ART DIRECTOR: Joan Curtis

CLIENT: St. Louis Galleria

MEDIUM: Pastel on Pastel Cloth

SIZE: 10x10

404

ARTIST: **WENDELL MINOR**

ART DIRECTOR: Al Cetta

CLIENT: HarperCollins Publishers

MEDIUM: Acrylic on Masonite

SIZE: 12x25

405

ARTIST: **DAN ANDREASEN**

ART DIRECTOR: Dan Forst

CLIENT: American Greetings

MEDIUM: Oil on Board

SIZE: 12x7

406

ARTIST: **GREG SPALENKA**

ART DIRECTOR: Silas Rhodes

CLIENT: School of Visual Arts

MEDIUM: Collage, Paint, Glue on Board

SIZE: 45x30

402

403

404

405

406

407

ARTIST: **GREG TESS**

ART DIRECTOR: Greg Tess

CLIENT: Pen Station

MEDIUM: Mixed Media

SIZE: 24x18

408

ARTIST: **ROBERT G. STEELE**

ART DIRECTOR: Andrew Danish

CLIENT: Stanford Alumni Assoc.

MEDIUM: Watercolor, Gouache on Paper

SIZE: 10x16

409

ARTIST: **JOHN COLLIER**

ART DIRECTOR: Richard Solomon

MEDIUM: Pastel

SIZE: 29x19

410

ARTIST: **JERRY LOFARO**

ART DIRECTOR: Francis Klaess

CLIENT: New Castle Arts, Ltd.

MEDIUM: Acrylic on Masonite

SIZE: 27x19

407

408

409

410

411

ARTIST: **SARAH WALDRON**

ART DIRECTOR: Sarah Waldron

MEDIUM: Oil on Paper

SIZE: 17x20

412

ARTIST: **REGAN DUNNICK**

ART DIRECTOR: Mitsutoshi Hosaka

CLIENT: Matsuzaki Shoji

MEDIUM: Pastel on Watercolor Paper

SIZE: 15x14

413

ARTIST: **SARAH WALDRON**

ART DIRECTOR: Sarah Waldron

MEDIUM: Oil on Paper

SIZE: 15x19

414

ARTIST: **DON IVAN PUNCHATZ**

ART DIRECTOR: John Isely

CLIENT: Medical Heritage Gallery

MEDIUM: Acrylic on Mylar Film

SIZE: 11x15

411

412

413

414

415

ARTIST: **RAUL COLON**

ART DIRECTOR: Tom Bricker

CLIENT: Johnson & Higgins

MEDIUM: Colored Pencils on Paper

SIZE: 12x10

416

ARTIST: **RICHARD BERNAL**

ART DIRECTOR: Pat Henning

CLIENT: Arts and Education Council of St. Louis

MEDIUM: Oil on Board

SIZE: 14x35

417

ARTIST: **JAMES McMULLAN**

ART DIRECTOR: Ellen Sorrin

CLIENT: New York City Ballet

MEDIUM: Watercolor on Paper

SIZE: 10x5

418

ARTIST: **JAMES McMULLAN**

ART DIRECTOR: Bill Freeland

CLIENT: LaGuardia Community College

MEDIUM: Watercolor on Paper

SIZE: 8x6

415

416

417

418

419

ARTIST: **GEORGE ABE**

ART DIRECTOR: Ken Lotz

CLIENT: Home Capitol

MEDIUM: Acrylic on Paper

SIZE: 20x15

420

ARTIST: **KAZUHIKO SANO**

ART DIRECTOR: Kazuhiko Sano

MEDIUM: Acrylic

SIZE: 19x17

421

ARTIST: **DUGALD STERMER**

ART DIRECTOR: Kit Hinrichs, Mike Hicks

CLIENT: Simpson Paper

MEDIUM: Graphite, Watercolor on Paper

SIZE: 15x12

422

ARTIST: **DUGALD STERMER**

ART DIRECTOR: Leslie Avchen

CLIENT: Consolidated Paper

MEDIUM: Pencil, Watercolor on Paper

SIZE: 11x16

419

420

421

422

423
ARTIST: **C. MICHAEL DUDASH**
ART DIRECTOR: C. Michael Dudash
CLIENT: Substrates Limited Edition Prints
MEDIUM: Oil on Linen on Board
SIZE: 52x36

424
ARTIST: **JEFFREY SMITH**
ART DIRECTOR: Carol Carson
CLIENT: Scholastic, Inc.
MEDIUM: Watercolor on Paper
SIZE: 15x22

425
ARTIST: **C.F. PAYNE**
ART DIRECTOR: Richard Solomon
MEDIUM: Mixed Media
SIZE: 17x13

426
ARTIST: **ETIENNE DELESSERT**
ART DIRECTOR: Steven Doyle
AGENCY: Doyle-Drenttel
CLIENT: World Financial Center
MEDIUM: Watercolor
SIZE: 12x10

423

424

425

426

427

ARTIST: **GARY HEAD**

ART DIRECTOR: Gary Head

MEDIUM: Oil on Canvas

SIZE: 14x13

428

ARTIST: **MATT ZUMBO**

ART DIRECTOR: Matt Zumbo

MEDIUM: Mixed Media on Board

SIZE: 11x16

429

ARTIST: **GARY HEAD**

ART DIRECTOR: Nancy DeSousa

CLIENT: Hallmark Cards, Inc.

MEDIUM: Oil on Canvas

SIZE: 29x23

430

ARTIST: **MATT ZUMBO**

ART DIRECTOR: Kitty Seidelman

CLIENT: Entertaining Dates

MEDIUM: Mixed Media on Photograph

SIZE: 9x7

427

428

429

430

431

ARTIST: **MARCO VENTURA**

ART DIRECTOR: Jessica Weber

CLIENT: Typographers International Association

MEDIUM: Oil, Pencil on Paper

SIZE: 8x9

432

ARTIST: **JOHN RUSH**

ART DIRECTOR: Peter King

CLIENT: Stratus Computers

MEDIUM: Gouache, Acrylic on Board

SIZE: 23x23

433

ARTIST: **DAVID BARBER**

ART DIRECTOR: Nancy Suttles

CLIENT: Rowley Printing

MEDIUM: Watercolor, Gouache on Board

SIZE: 18x36

434

ARTIST: **STEVE JOHNSON**

ART DIRECTOR: Cliff Bachner

CLIENT: Metropolitan Life

MEDIUM: Oil on Watercolor Paper

SIZE: 14x22

431

432

433

434

435

ARTIST: **BILL JAMES**

ART DIRECTOR: Deborah Pinals

AGENCY: Critt Graham & Assoc.

CLIENT: Graphic Industries

SIZE: 24x18

436

ARTIST: **ELWOOD H. SMITH**

ART DIRECTOR: Frank Biancalana

CLIENT: Nutrasweet

MEDIUM: Watercolor, India Ink

SIZE: 14x10

437

ARTIST: **LANE DUPONT**

ART DIRECTOR: Lane Dupont

MEDIUM: Pencil, Ink, Gouache on Paper

SIZE: 9x6

438

ARTIST: **BILLY O'DONNELL**

ART DIRECTOR: Steve Hoffmann

CLIENT: Lang & Smith

MEDIUM: Oil, Pastel

SIZE: 20x37

435

436

437

438

439

ARTIST: **TERESA FASOLINO**

ART DIRECTOR: Silas Rhodes

CLIENT: School of Visual Arts

MEDIUM: Acrylic on Canvas

SIZE: 31x20

440

ARTIST: **MIKE BENNY**

ART DIRECTOR: Bob Beyn

AGENCY: Serapheyn Beyn

CLIENT: Citizens Utililty Company

MEDIUM: Acrylic, Oil on Board

SIZE: 12x14

441

ARTIST: **MIKE BENNY**

ART DIRECTOR: Mike Benny

CLIENT: Sacramento Illustrators Guild

MEDIUM: Acrylic, Oil on Board

SIZE: 23x17

442

ARTIST: **RAFAL OLBINSKI**

ART DIRECTOR: Rafal Olbinski

MEDIUM: Acrylic on Canvas

SIZE: 35x24

439

440

441

442

443
ARTIST: **MICHAEL HALBERT**
ART DIRECTOR: Paul Harmon
CLIENT: Anheuser-Busch
MEDIUM: Scratchboard, Cotton Paper
SIZE: 20x15

444
ARTIST: **WARREN GEBERT**
ART DIRECTOR: Kathy Grubb
AGENCY: Gray Baumgarten Layport, Inc.
CLIENT: Parker/Hunter Inc.
MEDIUM: Pastel, Tempera
SIZE: 8x13

445
ARTIST: **STEVE JOHNSON**
ART DIRECTOR: Doug Joseph
CLIENT: Lincoln Bancorp
MEDIUM: Oil on Watercolor Paper
SIZE: 16x12

446
ARTIST: **STEVE JOHNSON**
ART DIRECTOR: Doug Joseph
CLIENT: Lincoln Bancorp
MEDIUM: Oil on Watercolor Paper
SIZE: 16x12

443

444

445

446

447

ARTIST: **JACK UNRUH**

ART DIRECTOR: Danny Kamerath

MEDIUM: Ink, Watercolor on Board

SIZE: 17x13

448

ARTIST: **ERIC DINYER**

ART DIRECTOR: Eric Dinyer

MEDIUM: Oil on Canvas

SIZE: 23x25

449

ARTIST: **CRAIG FRAZIER**

ART DIRECTOR: Craig Frazier

CLIENT: Friday Night Live (Marin Public Schools)

MEDIUM: Cut Amerlith and Xerox

SIZE: 34x24

450

ARTIST: **EVERETT PECK**

ART DIRECTOR: Richard W. Salzman

MEDIUM: Silkscreen on T-Shirt

SIZE: 10x8

KATMANDU • AUG. 3 • 1989   on owr way to zons 35 - owr guide is GØRAKHPUR

N • E • P • A • L •

447

448

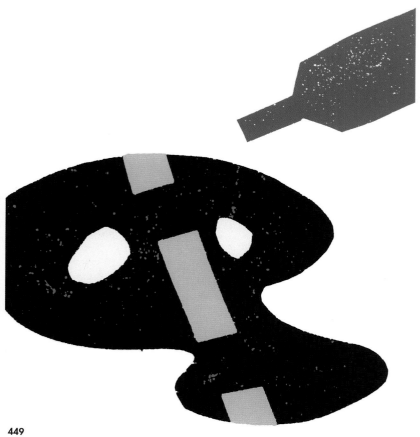

449

450

451

ARTIST: **SANDRA SPEIDEL**

ART DIRECTOR: Sandra McMillan

CLIENT: Marcel Schurman Cards

MEDIUM: Pastel, Watercolor on Paper

SIZE: 18x11

452

ARTIST: **WILSON McLEAN**

ART DIRECTOR: Alma Phipps

CLIENT: Chief Executive

MEDIUM: Oil on Canvas

SIZE: 20x30

453

ARTIST: **ROBERT HUNT**

ART DIRECTOR: Robert Hunt

MEDIUM: Oil, Pastel on Paper

SIZE: 38x25

454

ARTIST: **HAYES HENDERSON**

ART DIRECTOR: Hayes Henderson

CLIENT: Lincoln Gallery

MEDIUM: Oil

SIZE: 14x11

451

452

453

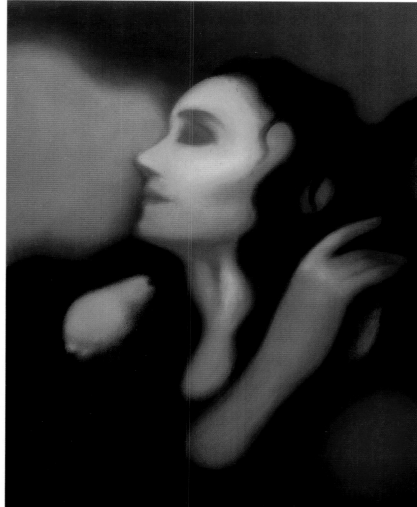

454

455

ARTIST: **GEORGE S. GAADT**

ART DIRECTOR: Robert Wages

CLIENT: Neenah Paper Co.

MEDIUM: Acrylic on Canvas Board

SIZE: 20x13

456

ARTIST: **DAVID GROVE**

ART DIRECTOR: David Grove

CLIENT: San Francisco Society of Illustrators

MEDIUM: Gouache, Acrylic on Board

SIZE: 12x18

457

ARTIST: **BART FORBES**

ART DIRECTOR: Bart Forbes

CLIENT: Mohawk Paper Co.

MEDIUM: Oil on Canvas

SIZE: 21x16

455

456

457

458

ARTIST: **BART FORBES**

ART DIRECTOR: Bart Forbes

CLIENT: Boston Athletic Association

MEDIUM: Oil on Canvas

SIZE: 40x24

458

N

E

W

V

I

S

I

O

N

S

NEW VISIONS

The work in this year's New Visions is a testament to the constant rejuvenation of the profession. The ninety-eight works of startling quality, technical proficiency, and imagination were selected for the Society of Illustrators Annual Student Scholarship Competition. We have included them in this year's Annual Book so that you may see the future in the hands of these talented young artists.

Over four thousand entries poured in from eighty excellent and highly directed, college-level art and design schools from across the country. Beverly Sacks was instrumental in the fund-raising for these awards, and Eileen Hedy Schultz guided the judges through the lengthy process of selection and from those entries the best were chosen to hang in the galleries of the Society of Illustrators Museum of American Illustration.

In addition to the technical skills being taught in today's art schools, the young people are also being trained in the business of illustration and, as shown in the work submitted for this exhibition, they are getting a taste of competition. And competition is what each and every illustrator working today must face.

We trust you will enjoy the promise of the future in New Visions.

ANNUAL SCHOLARSHIP COMPETITION

Congratulations to all of you in the 1991 Annual Scholarship Competition! You have just taken your first step toward becoming a professional illustrator. This first step is very important because the distance you must travel to achieve your goals as a professional will take patience, diligence, faith and common sense!

The road to self-discovery and search for an individual style will take long-range vision, so keep your sights fixed firmly on the road and *beware* of detours!

A very special thanks to Eileen Hedy Schultz and Beverly Sacks, co-chairmen of the Scholarship Committee, for doing a splendid job. Beverly also deserves kudos for her inspired work as chairman of the Annual Christmas Auction. The auction is a major fundraiser for scholarship programs.

I would like to thank the Hallmark Corporate Foundation for its continued support, along with The Starr Foundation, The Reader's Digest Association, Jellybean Photographics, The Norman Rockwell Museum at Stockbridge, Hachette Magazines, Comp 24/Color to Color, Air & Space Magazine, Paragon House and the family of Meg Wohlberg.

All of us at the Society of Illustrators wish all Student Scholarship Exhibitors a great future in the field of professional illustration . . . and when that time comes, we will welcome your membership application to join the Society!

Sincerely,

Wendell Minor
President

To the students whose work was selected this year—my *heartiest* congratulations!

To the students whose work was not selected this year—there were 4,220 entries from 80 colleges, along with excellent but very tough jurors, so don't lose heart.

To the 16 jurors and committee members who spent four days judging the entries (four judges per day), and another evening selecting award winners, a warm thank you for your time, your energy, and your expertise given!

To the parents, guardians, families, and friends of all students—our deepest gratitude for your unequalled support, not only of the students, but of the profession of illustration as well.

And to the instructors of these students—congratulations are long overdue. It's you who inspire, who encourage, who guide, and who pass along the expertise and knowledge that only years in the profession can bring.

Continued success and prosperity to you all!

Eileen Hedy Schultz
Co-Chairman, Education Committee

THE AWARDS

◀
Carl Square
Bruce Sharp, Instructor
Art Institute of Seattle
$2,500 Robert H. Blattner Award

▼
Madeline Aronson
Morton Kaish, Instructor
Fashion Institute of Technology
$2,000 Jellybean Photographics Award

▲
John Baranowski
Linda Benson, Instructor
School of Visual Arts
$2,000 The Starr Foundation Award

▲
Jason Dowd
Donald Puttman, Instructor
Art Center College of Design
$2,000 The Reader's Digest Association Award

▲
Michael Koelsch
Craig Nelson, Instructor
Art Center College of Design
$2,000 Albert Dorne Award

▲
John Ferry
Eric Dinyer, Instructor
Kansas City Art Institute
$2,000 The Starr Foundation Award

◀
Patrick Faricy
Will Cormier, Instructor
Art Center College of Design
$1,500 The Reader's Digest Association Award

▲
Cliff Towell
Jon McDonald, Instructor
Kendall College of Art & Design
$1,500 The Starr Foundation Award

◀
Matthew Walton
Sandy Appleoff, Instructor
Kansas City Art Institute
$1,500 Albert Dorne Award

◄
James Baran
Peter Caras, Instructor
duCret School of the Arts
$1,000 Jellybean Photographics Award

▼
Jacquelin Dyer
Jon McDonald, Instructor
Kendall College of Art & Design
$1,000 Award in memory of Jim Dickerson

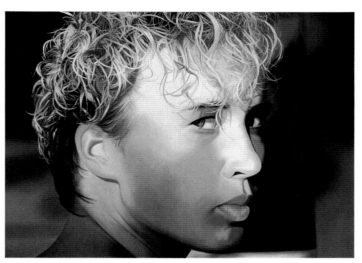

▲
James Bernardin
William Maughan, Instructor
Art Center College of Design
$1,000 Award in memory of Harry Rosenbaum

►
Chadd Ferron
Mark Hazlerig, Instructor
Columbus College of Art and Design
$1,000 Award in memory of Meg Wohlberg

▶
Danielle Nance
Jon McDonald, Instructor
Kendall College of Art & Design
$1,000 Comp 24/Color to Color Award

▲
Ethan Long
Laurence Kresek, Instructor
Ringling School of Art and Design
$1,000 Friends of the Institute of Commercial Art Award

▼
Dawn James
Jon McDonald, Instructor
Kendall College of Art & Design
$1,000 The Norman Rockwell Museum at Stockbridge Award

▲
Francisco Mora
Phil Hays, Instructor
Art Center College of Design
$1,000 Hachette Magazines Award

▼
Howard Porter
Ken Davies, Instructor
Paier College of Art
$1,000 Albert Dorne Award

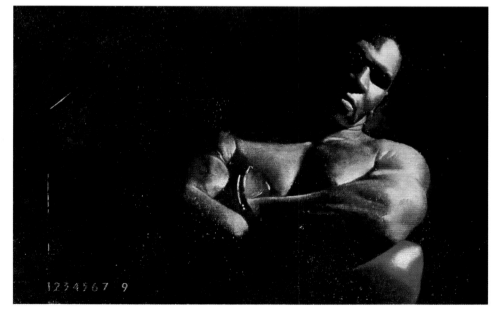

▲
Scott Medlock
Richard Bunkall, Instructor
Art Center College of Design
$1,000 Acryla Weave, Inc. Award

Angeline Shearstone
Doug Andersen, Instructor
University of Hartford
$1,000 Kirchoff/Wohlberg Award
in memory of Frances Means

Terry Wetmore
Bunny Carter, Instructor
San Jose State University
$1,000 The Norman Rockwell Museum
at Stockbridge Award

Eleni Symeonoglou
Patti Bellantoni, Instructor
School of Visual Arts
Paragon House Commission Award

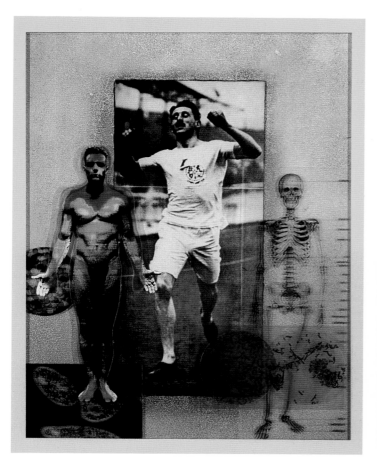

◄
David Kahl
Robert Rodriguez, Instructor
Art Center College of Design
$500 Effie Bowie Award

▲
Kazushige Nitta
Sal Catalano, Instructor
School of Visual Arts
Air & Space Magazine Commission Award

◄
Jess Mueller
Rich Kryczka, Instructor
American Academy of Art
$500 Award in memory of Melanie Doolittle

T H E   E X H I B I T I O N

1 Stella Arbelaez
Jane Bixby-Weller, Instructor
Fashion Institute of Technology

2 Kim Baker
Richard Hull, Instructor
Brigham Young University

3 John Baranowski
Linda Benson, Instructor
School of Visual Arts

4 Kristen Battafarano
David Christiana, Instructor
Northern Arizona University

5 Sean Beavers
Sal Catalano, Instructor
School of Visual Arts

6 Christopher Bolles
Tim O'Brien, Instructor
The University of the Arts

7 Rich Bowman
Eric Dinyer, Instructor
Kansas City Art Institute

8 Cheryl Briscoe
Garry Colby, Instructor
Center for Creative Studies

9 Simeen Brown
Richard Hull, Instructor
Brigham Young University

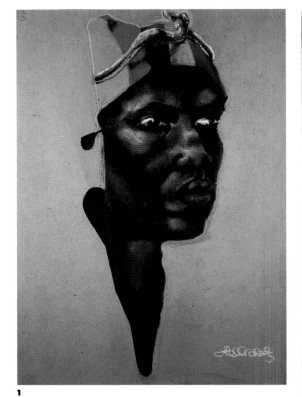

1

2

3

4

5

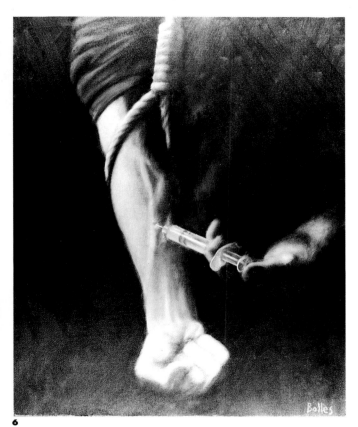

6

9

7

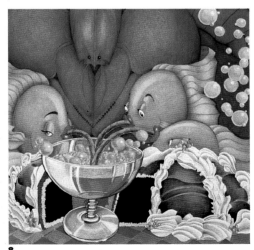

8

11

10

12

13

14

16

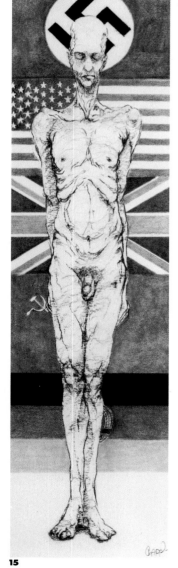

15

17

18

19

21

20

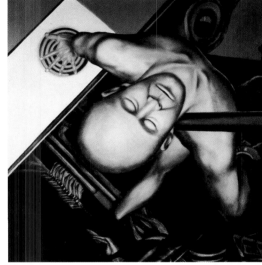

22

24

23

25

26

28

29

27

30

31

32

33

36

37

34

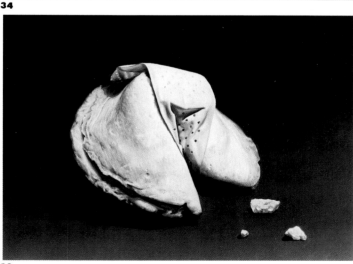

38

35

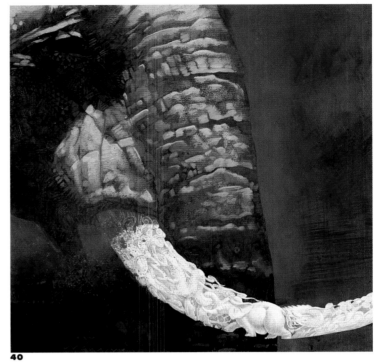

40

39

41

42

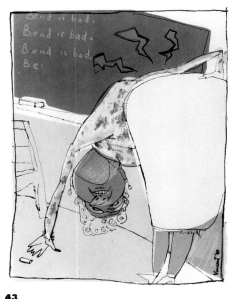

43

46

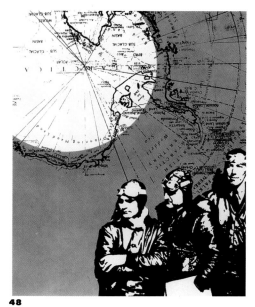

48

44

47

45

49

50

52

54

51

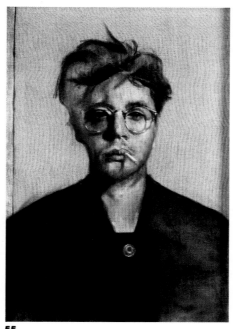

55

56

53

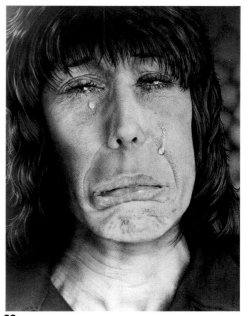

58

59

57

60

62

61

63

64

66

65

69

67

68

70

71

75

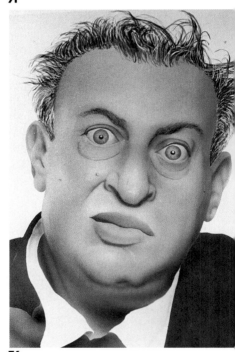

76

72

79

74

78

77

73

81

80

82

84

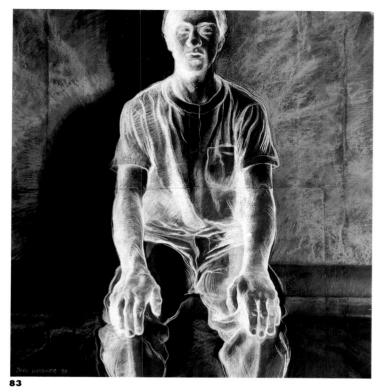

83

85

86

88

87

89

90

91

92

93

94

97

98

95

96

ACKNOWLEDGEMENTS

Jury

Paul Bacon	Eugene Light
Richard Berenson	Anita Marci
Bill Charmatz	Abby Merrill
Peter Fiore	Doreen Minuto
Bruce Hall	Agnes Orioles
Catherine Huerta	Jim Sharpe
Dennis Kendrick	Scott Snow
David Lewis	Bob Ziering

Special Topics Selection Jury

Mitchell Hooks	Susan Newman
Louis Kolenda	Eileen Hedy Schultz
Al Lorenz	

Committee

Eileen Hedy Schultz, *Co-Chair*	Richard Berenson
	Peter Fiore
Beverly Sacks, *Co-Chair*	Al Lorenz

Administration

Terrence Brown	Phyllis Harvey
Ray Alma	Clare McLean
Lillian Grossman	Norma Pimsler

Hallmark Corporate Foundation Matching Grants

The Hallmark Corporate Foundation of Kansas City, Missouri, is again this year supplying full matching grants for all of the awards in the Society's Student Scholarship Competition. Grants, restricted to the Illustration Departments, are awarded to the following institutions:

$9,000 Art Center College of Design

$4,500 Kendall College of Art & Design

$3,500 Kansas City Art Institute

$2,500 Art Institute of Seattle

$2,000 Fashion Institute of Technology

$2,000 School of Visual Arts

$1,000 Columbus College of Art and Design

$1,000 duCret School of the Arts

$1,000 University of Hartford

$1,000 Paier College of Art

$1,000 Ringling School of Art and Design

$1,000 San Jose State University

$500 American Academy of Art

ARTIST INDEX

ART DIRECTORS, CLIENTS, AGENCIES

PROFESSIONAL STATEMENTS

Camille Przewodek

Robert Cunningham

Robert Crawford

Joel Spector

ERFORMANCE

Bill James

Braldt Bralds

In 1990, six illustrators with divergent styles were each provided with an Alfa Romeo 164 and asked to illustrate their impressions of the car for an advertising campaign.

The campaign was designed to uniquely present the 164 as a distinctive and desirable automobile.

The consumer response to the first two completed ads totaled over 23,000 requests for additional information on the 164 and over 11,000 requests for prints of the main illustrations.

The power and style of the illustrations made an overwhelming success of the campaign perfectly in tune with the image of Alfa Romeo.

To get in touch with any of these high performers call Charlotte at 203-868-7577 or by fax 203-868-7060.

FRED OTNES

COLLAGE AND ASSEMBLAGE

REPRESENTED BY BILL ERLACHER / ARTISTS ASSOCIATES / 211 EAST 51 STREET / NEW YORK, NY / 10019 / TEL · (212) 755-1365/6

R O B E R T   H U N T

S T U D I O :   4 1 5   4 5 9   6 8 8 2

REPRESENTED BY BARBARA GORDON 212 686-3514

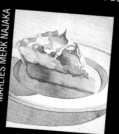

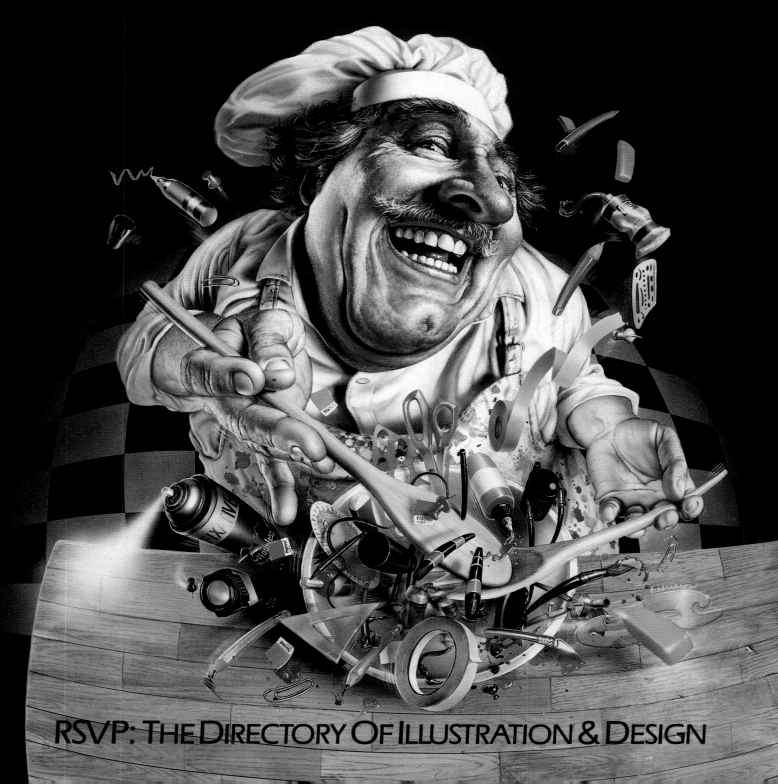

ARTCO

Gail Thurm and Jeff Palmer
Tammy Shannon, Associate

Serving New York City clients:
232 Madison Avenue, Suite 600, New York, New York 10016 (212) 889-8777, FAX: (212) 447-1475

Serving clients outside New York City:
227 Godfrey Road, Weston, Connecticut 06883 (203) 222-8777, FAX: (203) 454-9940

Additional work may be seen in American Showcase Vols. 10, 11, 12, 13, 14 and 15.

Jean Restivo—Monti

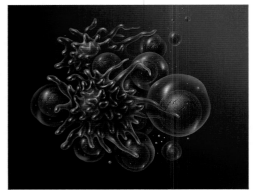

Edmond Alexander

Oren Sherman

Mark Smollin

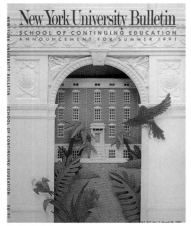

Sally Vitsky

Michael Heslop

Lisa Henderling

Ed Gazsi

Alan & Beau Daniels

Dan Brown

ARTCO brings quality award-winning illustration to a variety of projects in a
wide range of areas including advertising, book publishing, magazine publishing, corporate literature and annual reports.

Jeff Cornell

Alain Chang

Gene Boyer

David Loew

Cynthia Turner

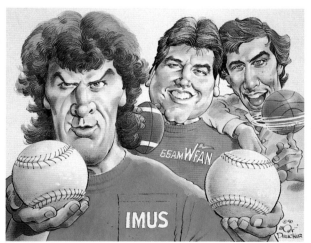

Mort Drucker

Rick McCollum

Joann Daley

Paul Sheldon

Ed Acuna

George Angelini

Peter **Fiore**

"**W***hy talk when you can paint?*"

Milton Avery

Broeck **Steadman**

Brad **Teare**

Artists
Representative

270
Park Avenue So.
Suite 10B

New York
New York
10010

212
260-4153
260-4358 Fax

Sandra **Filippucci**

Deborah **Chabrian**

Paul **Bachem**

Contact: *Peter*   *Betty*
              Schlegel   *Krichman*

Times Change . . . Styles Change . .

Illustration by
MEG WOHLBERG

Kirchoff/Wohlberg . . . . . . Representing

Kirchoff/Wohlberg, Inc. • 897 Boston Post Road • Madison, CT 06443 • (203) 245-7308

Illustration Copyright © 1990 FLOYD COOPER
From Laura Charlotte, Published by Philomel Books

Illustrators For Six Decades

Artists Representatives • 866 United Nations Plaza • New York, NY 10017 • (212) 644-2020

JEFF MANGIAT

BOB TANENBAUM

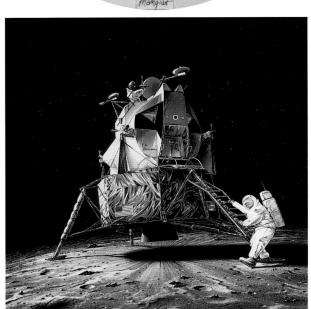

30th ANNIVERSARY MENDOLA LTD. 1961 1991

CHARLES LIESE

BILL JAMES

30th ANNIVERSARY MENDOLA LTD. 1961 1991

BILL VANN

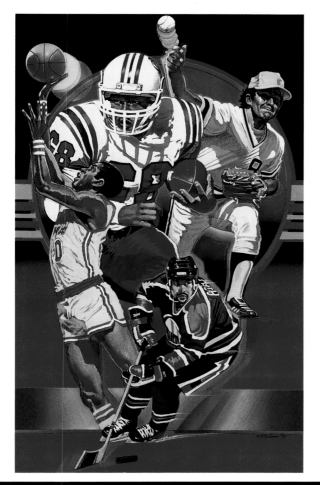

SCHWAB

PERKINS SHEARER
11TH ANNUAL
POLO CUP

HIGHLANDS RANCH

RENARD REPRESENTS
212/490-2450

FORBES

RODRIGUEZ

RUDNAK

MARTIN

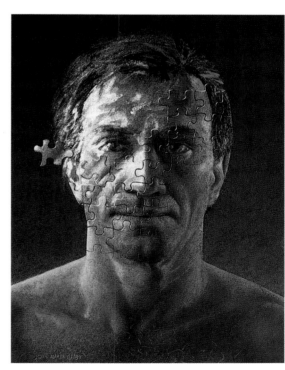

RENARD REPRESENTS
212/490-2450

OVER

1991
Carl Square
Society of Illustrators
Robert H. Blattner Award

AND OVER

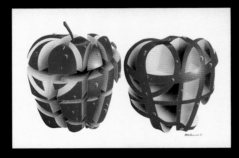

1988
Mike Rasciner
Society of Illustrators
Starr Foundation Award

AND OVERACHIEVERS.

1987
John Wheaton
Society of Illustrators
Starr Foundation Award

Competitions show year after year what we do every day.

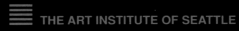

THE ART INSTITUTE OF SEATTLE

2323 Elliott Avenue
Seattle, Washington 98121
1-800-275-2471

Society of Illustrators
Museum Shop

The Society of Illustrators Museum of American Illustration maintains a shop featuring many quality products. Four-color, large format books document contemporary illustration and the great artists of the past. Catalogues from museum exhibitions highlight specific artists, eras and publications. The Business Library is a must for professionals, young or established. Museum quality prints and posters capture classic images, most available only through The Museum Shop. T-shirts and sweatshirts make practical and fun gifts.

The Museum Shop is an extension of the Society's role as the center for illustration in America today. For further information or quantity discounts, contact the Society at TEL:(212) 838-2560
FAX: (212) 838-2561

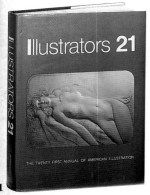

1
ILLUSTRATORS 21
$20.00

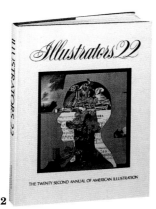

2
ILLUSTRATORS 22
$20.00

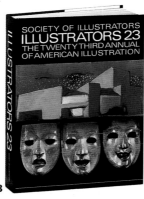

3
ILLUSTRATORS 23
$20.00

4
ILLUSTRATORS 24
$20.00

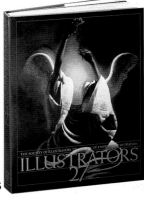

5
ILLUSTRATORS 27
$35.00

6
ILLUSTRATORS 28
$40.00

7
ILLUSTRATORS 29
$45.00

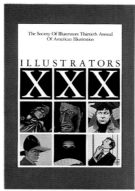

8
ILLUSTRATORS 30
$49.95

9
ILLUSTRATORS 31
$49.95

10
ILLUSTRATORS 32
$49.95

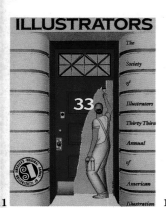

1
ILLUSTRATORS 33
$49.95

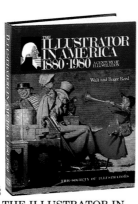

12
THE ILLUSTRATOR IN
AMERICA (1880-1980)
$40.00

13
20 YEARS OF AWARD
WINNERS
$30.00

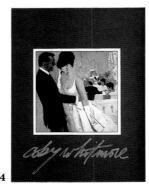

14
COBY WHITMORE-
.20pp. color. The good life of the
1950s and 1960s as illustrated
in Ladies's Home Journal,
McCall's and Redbook. $16.00

A limited number of copies of the Illustrators Annuals from 1959 to ILLUSTRATORS 20, also ILLUSTRATORS 25 and 26, are available, as is. Contact the Society for details. These volumes are out of print at this time.

FAX (212) 838-2561

EXHIBITION CATALOGUES These volumes have been created for exhibitions in the Society of Illustrators Museum of American Illustration. They focus on specific artists, eras or subjects.

15
Stevan Dohanos

STEVAN DOHANOS-
36pp, color.
The 1986 New Britain
Museum of American
Art retrospective of
the noted *Saturday
Evening Post* cover
artist. $5.00

16
ARTHUR I. KELLER -
36pp, B&W. A look
at The Belle Epoque
and its delineator.
$7.50

17
THE ARTIST EXPLORES
OUR WORLD - 32pp,
biographies of the 60
artists represented
in the *National
Geographic* centennial
exhibition. $5.00

18
AMERICA'S GREAT
WOMEN ILLUSTRATORS
(1850-1950) - 24 pp, B & W.
Decade by decade
essays by important
historians on
role of women in
illustration. $5.00

MUSEUM QUALITY PRINTS prints of classic works from the Society's Permanent Collection, reproduced on 100% acid free, 100 lb. rag paper in an 11 x 14 format. Suitable for framing. $12.00 per print; $38.00 for the set of four

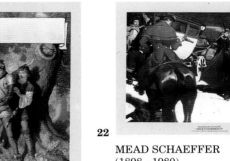

19
J.C. LEYENDECKER
(1874 -1951)

20
DEAN CORNWELL
(1892-1960)

21
N.C. WYETH
(1883 - 1945)

22
MEAD SCHAEFFER
(1898 - 1980)

THE BUSINESS LIBRARY Each of these volumes is a valuable asset to the professional artist whether established or just starting out. Together they form a solid base for your business.

**THE BUSINESS LIBRARY -
The set of three
volumes - $33.00**

23
GRAPHIC ARTISTS
GUILD HANDBOOK,
PRICING AND ETHICAL
GUIDELINES -
7th Edition - 1991
Includes an outline of
ethical standards and
business practices, as well
as price ranges for
hundreds of uses and
sample contracts.
$22.95

24
THE LEGAL GUIDE
FOR
THE VISUAL ARTIST-
Tad Crawford's text
explains basic
copyrights, moral rights,
the sale of
rights, taxation,
business accounting and
the legal support groups
available to artists.
1989 Edition. $18.95

25
HEALTH HAZARDS
MANUAL-
A comprehensive review of
materials and supplies,
from fixatives to pigments,
airbrushes to solvents.
$3.50

ANNUAL EXHIBITION POSTERS The "Call for Entries" poster created each year for the Society's Annual Exhibition. $3.00 each

26
21st Annual-
BOB PEAK
"The Year of the
Horse"

27
25th Annual-
BOB HEINDEL
"Dancer"

28
29th Annual-HODGES
SOILEAU "The
Palette"

29
32nd Annual-
ROGER HUYSSEN/
GERARD HUERTA
"Golden Anniversary"

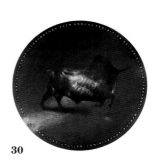

30
34th Annual-
BRAD HOLLAND
"Brahma Bull"

OTHER ARTISTS AVAILABLE: **31.** 26th Annual - Marvin Mattelson "The Unknown Illustrator" **32.** 27th Annual - BARRON STOREY "1984" **33.** 30th Annual - DAVID GROVE "Dreaming" **34.** 31st Annual - BOB McGINNIS "Farmhouse" **35.** 33rd Annual - HERB TAUSS "Memories"

SPECIAL EVENT AND EXHIBITION POSTERS

36
Homage to Howard Pyle-
The Society's 75th
Anniversary" by FRED
OTNES

37
"The Illustrator in America
(1880-1890)" by
NORMAN ROCKWELL and
MARK ENGLISH

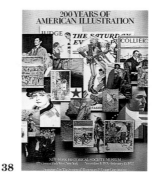

38
"200 Years of American
Illustration" by
FRED OTNES

39
"Twenty Years of Award Winners"
by MURRAY TINKELMAN

40
"The Rodeo Painted"
by WALT SPITZMILLER

OTHER ARTISTS AVAILABLE: **41.** "Visions of Flight" by DAVID K. STONE **42.** "Prizefighters" by BOB PEAK **43.** "Humor" by LOU BROOKS **44.** "The Artist Explores our World" by NED SEIDLER. $5.00 each **45.** "The Fires of Imagination" by BRAD HOLLAND **46.** "Hearthland" by Wendell Minor **47.** "The 15th at Oakmont" by DON MOSS **48.** "The Illustrator and the Environment" by FOLON. $10.00 each

---

PRINTS FROM THE HOTEL BARMEN'S ASSOCIATION OF TOKYO CALENDARS These full-color lithographs feature prominent American illustrators interpreting popular cocktails. $5.00 per print

49
GARY KELLEY
"Black Russian"

50
ROBERT GIUSTI
"Americano"

51
BOB PEAK
"Blue Sapphire"

52
MARK ENGLISH
"Angel's Kiss"

53
DOUG JOHNSON
"Irish Coffee"

OTHER ARTISTS AVAILABLE: **54.** ALAN E. COBER "Pousse Cafe" **55.** BRAD HOLLAND "Tequila Sunrise" **56.** JIM McMULLAN "Whiskey Sour" **57.** MURRAY TINKELMAN "Champagne Cocktail"

SI T-SHIRTS Incorporating the Society's logo in three designs (multiple logo, words and lines, large SI). Orange shirts with black lettering. Blue shits with white lettering. White shirts with two color lettering. $ 8.00 each. SIZES: Small, Large, X-Large. Also special heavyweight cotton, four-color T-shirts featuring classic images from the Society's Permanent Collection: $ 20.00 each. Sizes: Large, X-Large (61-62)

58

59

60

61

"Easter"
by J.C. LEYENDECKER
The Saturday Evening Post, 1934

62

"The Black Arrow"
by N.C. WYETH
Frontispiece for the
Scribner's Classic by
Robert Louis Stevenson

SI SWEATSHIRTS Blue with white lettering of multiple logo. Grey with large SI. $ 20.00 each. Sizes: Large, X-Large, XX-Large

63

65

64

SI LAPEL PINS $6.00 Actual Size

The Society's famous Red and Black logo, designed by Bradbury Thompson, is featured on the following gift items:

65. Ceramic coffee mugs - heavyweight 14 oz mugs are white with the two-color logo *$ 6.00 each $ 20.00 for a set of 4*

66. Blue corduroy baseball caps - adjustable back strap and the logo in white *$ 15.00*

67. Tote bags - Heavyweight, white canvas bags are 14" high with the two-color logo *$ 15.00*

ORDER FORM

ENCLOSED IS MY CHECK FOR $_____

Please make check payable to Society of Illustrators

Name
Company
Street
City
State   Zip

Please charge my credit card:

❏ American Express   ❏ Master Card   ❏ Visa

Card Number
Expiration date
Signature

Qty	Item #	Price
	1	$20.00
	2	$20.00
	3	$20.00
	4	$20.00
	5	$35.00
	6	$40.00
	7	$45.00
	8	$49.95
	9	$49.95
	10	$49.95
	11	$49.95
	12	$40.00

Qty	Item #	Price
	13	$30.00
	14	$16.00
	15	$ 5.00
	16	$ 7.50
	17	$ 5.00
	18	$ 5.00
	19	$12.00
	20	$12.00
	21	$12.00
	22	$12.00
	23	$22.95
	24	$18.95

Qty	Item #	Price
	25	$ 3.50
	26	$ 5.00
	27	$ 5.00
	28	$ 5.00
	29	$ 5.00
	30	$ 5.00
	31	$ 5.00
	32	$ 5.00
	33	$ 5.00
	34	$ 5.00
	35	$ 5.00
	36	$ 5.00

Qty	Item #	Price
	37	$ 5.00
	38	$ 5.00
	39	$ 5.00
	40	$10.00
	41	$ 5.00
	42	$ 5.00
	43	$ 5.00
	44	$ 5.00
	45	$10.00
	46	$10.00
	47	$10.00
	48	$10.00

Qty	Item #	Price
	49	$ 5.00
	50	$ 5.00
	51	$ 5.00
	52	$ 5.00
	53	$ 5.00
	54	$ 5.00
	55	$ 5.00
	56	$ 5.00
	57	$ 5.00

Qty	Item#	Price	
	58	$8.00	
Color	Orange	Blue	White
Size	Small	Large	X-Large
	59	$8.00	
Color	Orange	Blue	White
Size	Small	Large	X-Large
	60	$8.00	
Color	Orange	Blue	White
Size	Small	Large	X-Large
	61	$20.00	
	62	$20.00	
	Large	X-Large	

Qty	Item#	Price	
	63	$20.00	
Color	Blue	Grey	
Size	Large	X-Large	XX-Large Blue Only
	64	$6.00	
	65	$6.00	
	Set of 4	$20.00	
	66	$15.00	
	67	$15.00	

	68	Business Library - **23, 24 & 25** $33.00
	69	Set of Four Prints - **19, 20, 21 & 22** $15.00

Total price of item(s) ordered: _____

shipping/handling per order: $3.50

TOTAL DUE: _____